READING SCRIPTURE
AS WESLEYANS

Reading Scripture as Wesleyans

Joel B. Green

Abingdon Press
Nashville

READING SCRIPTURE AS WESLEYANS

Copyright © 2010 by Abingdon Press

All rights reserved.

This book is printed on acid-free paper.

Library of Congress Cataloging-in-Publication Data

Green, Joel B., 1956-
    Reading Scripture as Wesleyans / Joel B. Green.
      p. cm.
    Includes bibliographical references (p.   ) and index.
    ISBN 978-1-4267-0691-2 (trade pbk. : alk. paper)
    1. Bible. N.T.—Criticism, interpretation, etc. 2. Wesley, John, 1703–1791.   I. Title.
    BS2361.3.G74 2010
    225.6088'287—dc22

                             2010002087

10 11 12 13 14 15 16 17 18 19—10 9 8 7 6 5 4 3 2 1

MANUFACTURED IN THE UNITED STATES OF AMERICA

Contents

Introduction

For the heirs of John Wesley—I will call them "methodists"[1] — the central importance of Scripture in the formation of God's people is nonnegotiable. Evidence for this claim in Wesley is easy to document. Consider Wesley's own words: "Bring me plain, scriptural proof for your assertion, or I cannot allow it."[2] "You are in danger of enthusiasm every hour if you depart ever so little from Scripture."[3] In his eighteenth-century Britain, Wesley and his movement were slandered for their emphasis on Scripture. Like rotten tomatoes, names like Bible-bigots and Bible-moths were tossed at them by their detractors.[4] Wesley wore these derisive words as badges of honor.

As important as Scripture is within the Wesleyan tradition, though, I do not think I am exaggerating much when I suggest that methodists have not always known what to do with Scripture. More particularly, we have not always known what to do with Scripture as *methodists*. We have tended in recent decades, for example, either to follow the patterns of reading the biblical materials taught and learned in universities and seminaries, or to reject those patterns. Neither approach is particularly methodist. Neither leads to our reading Scripture as Wesleyans.

I will of course have far more to say about this in the chapters that follow, but let me provide some initial hints here. Simply put, the typical patterns of reading the biblical materials taught and learned in formal biblical studies today have little to do with reading the Bible in and for the church, methodist or otherwise. In fact, one of the hallmarks of the reigning approach to biblical studies has been its requirement that practitioners put their faith commitments on hold. Serious biblical studies, according to this approach, neither assumes nor necessarily leads to religious commitments. This is not to say that these patterns of biblical study ought to be rejected wholesale, but it is to say that, left to themselves, these interpretive practices have little to do with the life of the people called methodists. As I have just suggested, the answer does not lie in rejecting this sort of disciplined approach to the Bible in favor of what is sometimes called "taking the Bible literally." Wesley made a number of assumptions about the nature of Scripture, and these led to characteristic practices for reading the Bible. The result could hardly be called "precritical" or "naive."

We find one of the most telling comments Wesley made about the Bible in the opening to his "Sermons on Several Occasions":

> I want to know one thing, the way to heaven—how to land safe on that happy shore. God himself has condescended to teach the way: for this very end he came from heaven. He has written it down in a book. O give me that book! At any price give me the Book of God! I have it. Here is knowledge enough for me. Let me be *homo unius libri* [a person of one book]. Here then I am, far from the busy ways of others. I sit down alone: only God is here. In his presence I open, I read his Book—for this end, to find the way to heaven.[5]

Wesley urges in no uncertain terms that the aim of Scripture is to lead us to and in "the way to heaven." We might take exception to the way Wesley has thus described biblical interpretation as something he does "alone." We might also take exception to the fact that someone who wrote so many books and who was himself so widely read could thus aim to be "a person of one book."[6] In the pages that follow, we will see how Wesley's practice as a reader of Scripture undermines these two criticisms. Clearly, when Wesley interpreted the Bible, he was never alone, but surrounded by other interpreters, contemporary and past. Moreover, as he worked with Scripture he drew on a wide range of learning—including commentaries and devotional works, which we might have expected, but also classical philosophers, early church writers, and the latest science of his day. These criticisms, then, should not detract from the central point of this passage from his

"Sermons on Several Occasions." This is that, for Wesley, reading Scripture is tied to the journey of salvation. The Bible teaches "the way to heaven." And Wesley reads the Bible with this aim in mind—"to find the way to heaven."

How do we know if the Bible is "true," then? If it shows us the way to heaven. How do we know if we have read the Bible well? If our reading of Scripture has furthered our progress on the way to heaven. "The way to heaven," of course, is for Wesley not simply a statement about eternal bliss. It refers more broadly to the journey of salvation—from original sin to justification and new birth, and on to holiness. Reading Scripture as Wesleyans means taking seriously both this aim of Scripture (to show the way to heaven) and these consequences of our reading Scripture (to find the way to heaven).

This also means that it is never enough to say that methodists "take the Bible seriously" or that we think "the Bible is important for faith and life." This would be true of Christians generally. More is at stake than these statements, however true they might be. To push further, we need to recognize that our heritage as Wesleyans is a tradition that underscores the importance of theological formation for biblical interpretation. As Wesleyans, we read with a constant eye to what Wesley called "the Scripture way of salvation." We read with a constant eye toward the ongoing formation of the people of God in holiness. There are other ways to read the Bible, to be sure. But methodists locate their reading of the Bible within the larger Wesleyan tradition. We read the Bible as Wesleyans. And we need to know what this looks like.

My focus in this book is the New Testament, and more particularly a sampling of New Testament books with which Wesley engaged in his preaching and his *Explanatory Notes upon the New Testament*. Generally, I have been less interested in what Wesley says about how he reads Scripture and more concerned with what he actually does as he reads Scripture. What motifs surface? What informs and shapes his interpretation? The result has been a fascinating exploration of how Wesley engaged in disciplined theological interpretation of Scripture. Here we see something of what it means to be Wesleyan—not in the sense of marching lockstep to his cadence or matching his gait with our own. Instead, we see how certain assumptions about the nature of Scripture and how certain commitments about the overall message or theme of Scripture might shape serious, engaged reading of the Bible. Here we see how we might exhibit in our interpretive practices and beliefs the distinctive keys of our methodist heritage.

I have cited Wesley's own words extensively, but in doing so have taken some liberties. I have edited for punctuation and archaic word usage, for example, as well as introduced gender-inclusive language in references to the human family. In each case, I have provided a reference back to Wesley's writings in order to aid those interested in consulting Wesley's original prose.

Unless indicated otherwise, biblical citations follow the NRSV.

Finally, let me express my genuine appreciation to Kathy Armistead, for extraordinary encouragement and behind-the-scenes support; to former colleagues—especially Ken Collins, Larry Wood, and Mike Pasquarello—for many a formative conversation; to Fuller Theological Seminary, for a sabbatical during which this book was completed and more generally for a community of friends among whom I have experienced remarkable hospitality; and especially to the fortnightly Theological Interpretation Reading Group, companions on the way to heaven.

1
Gospel of Matthew

The Gospel of Matthew, sometimes called the First Gospel on account of its position as the first of the Four Gospels, serves as a bridge between the Old and the New Testaments. As we turn the page from the end of the Old Testament to the beginning of the New, we find a startling continuity. Malachi 4:4-6 reads,

> Remember the teaching of my servant Moses, the statutes and ordinances that I commanded him at Horeb for all Israel.
>
> Lo, I will send you the prophet Elijah before the great and terrible day of the LORD comes. He will turn the hearts of parents to their children and the hearts of children to their parents, so that I will not come and strike the land with a curse.

First, like Moses, Jesus is threatened by a ruler and narrowly escapes, then returns from exile on divine instructions (Matt 2:13-21). As Moses received and delivered the Ten Commandments on Mount Sinai, so Jesus delivers his great Sermon on a mountain (Matt 5–7). And just as Moses' name is associated with the first five books of the OT, collectively labeled "the book of Moses" (see Mark 12:26), so Matthew provides five major blocks of Jesus' instruction (Matt 5–7; 10; 13; 18; 24–25). Second, prior to the public ministry of Jesus we read in Matthew's Gospel the story of John the Baptist (Matt 3), about whom Jesus later remarks, "He is Elijah who is to come" (11:14; see also 17:10-12). Clearly, the story of Jesus and his church is deeply rooted in the OT story of Israel, God's people.

John Wesley regarded the Gospel of Matthew as the "first"

Gospel in another sense. Following a long tradition, he considered it the first Gospel to have been written, and thought that the other Gospel writers, or Evangelists, knew the First Gospel and supplied what it had omitted.[1] Study of the Gospels since Wesley's day has tended in a different direction, identifying the Gospel of Mark both as the first to have been written and as a key source for Matthew's Gospel. Gospels study has also come to emphasize more that each Gospel has its own emphasis as it presents the significance of the one person, Jesus of Nazareth.[2] In fact, in Greek, the title of the Gospel of Matthew is simply "according to Matthew." This is because "gospel" or "good news" refers first to the advent of Jesus and only then to a kind of book that narrates the career of Jesus, focusing especially on his public ministry, his suffering and death, and the empty tomb.

Three Themes in Wesley's Reading of Matthew

We get a flavor of how Wesley interpreted the Gospel of Matthew by focusing on three aspects of his reading. First, *Jesus is the Christ,* about which Wesley writes:

> The word "Christ" in Greek and "Messiah" in Hebrew both signify "Anointed"—and imply the prophetic, priestly, and royal qualities that were to meet in the Messiah. Among the Jews, anointing was the ceremony whereby prophets, priests, and kings were initiated into those offices. And if we look into ourselves, we shall find our need of Christ in all three respects. We are by nature at a distance from God, alienated from God, and incapable of a free access to God. Hence, we need a Mediator, an Intercessor; in a word, we need Christ in his priestly office. This regards our state with respect to God. And with respect to ourselves, we find a total darkness, blindness, ignorance of God, and the things of God. Now here we want Christ in his prophetic office, to enlighten our minds, and teach us the whole will of God. We find also within us a strange misrule of appetites and passions. For these we want Christ in his royal character, to reign in our hearts, and subdue all things to himself.[3]

Wesley writes these words as a comment on the second appearance of the term "Messiah" in Matthew's Gospel, at the end of

Matthew's account of Jesus' lineage: "and Jacob the father of Joseph the husband of Mary, of whom Jesus was born, *who is called the Messiah*" (1:16, emphasis added). Matthew himself draws out the significance of Jesus' messiahship with reference to Jesus' royal status as the Son of God whose rejection by leaders in Jerusalem is central to his mission to bring salvation (e.g., 2:4-6; 16:16; 26–27). Wesley goes further, reflecting a working assumption that the Gospel of Matthew was written not only for a first-century audience but for the church of his day and ours.

This does not mean that he was simply interested in the question, What does this biblical text mean to me? Instead, he is trying to sort out what it means to call Jesus "Messiah" or "Christ" for the faith of the whole church. Note, then, that his reading is grounded in Israel's story in the OT and in the long-standing doctrinal interest in the "three offices" of Christ: Prophet, Priest, and King. We see in Wesley's reading his belief in the "simultaneity of Scripture"—that is, the ability of the one scriptural text to speak effectively at the same time to its original audience and to the church that identifies the Gospel of Matthew as its Scripture.

We can think about what Wesley is doing this way. According to a classical definition, the church is "one, holy, catholic (or universal), and apostolic." To say that the church is "one" is to admit that the people of God to whom Matthew first addressed his Gospel, the people of God in Wesley's day, the people of God in our day, and those who will be gathered as the end-time people of God are actually one people. There is only one church. So words addressed to God's people in the first century are actually addressed to the whole people of God, everywhere and at all times. And for this people, even the title given Jesus, "Christ," has immediate and far-reaching significance for identifying and addressing the human condition and faithful discipleship.

The second theme is the *kingdom of heaven*. The Gospel of Matthew tends to use this phrase where the Gospels of Mark and Luke have "kingdom of God." Wesley observes that "kingdom of heaven" and "kingdom of God" are simply two ways of referring to the same thing. One way to translate this might be "heavenly empire," though Wesley was clear that this was not simply "a future happy state in heaven." Nor is it our possession. Rather, the kingdom of heaven refers to the gathering of God's people, "subjects" of the kingdom, under the leadership of God's Son. Accordingly, Jesus' proclamation of the "heavenly empire" refers to the social order (Wesley calls it a "society") that would be formed by God's people first on earth and then with God in glory. The condition of entry into the kingdom is repentance, and for Wesley this demonstrated that the kingdom of heaven "was a spiritual kingdom, and that no wicked person, no matter how politic, brave, or learned, could possibly be a subject in it."[4] Wesley thus highlights what subsequent interpreters, including many contemporary readers, failed to grasp.

The centrality of God's dominion for Jesus' mission is hard to miss, given that Matthew mentions the kingdom more than fifty times in his Gospel. On this everyone agrees. More elusive has been a consensus around the nature of the kingdom. Wesley saw clearly, though, that the presence of a "kingdom" implied "subjects," and that this had immediate implications for social relations. Elsewhere, he works these out especially in terms of love of God and love of neighbor.

What Wesley did not take fully into account, though, is the relationship of the heavenly kingdom to all other "kingdoms." If our allegiance to God is primary and nonnegotiable, what bearing does this have for our relationships with all sorts of institutions that seek our reverence and obedience? This would have been crucial in the first-century Roman world, but it is an important question for us, too.

Third, it is interesting to find Wesley thinking about the relationship of *Christian Scripture and modern science*. In his reading of the First Gospel, questions about science and theology surfaced because of Jesus' miracles. In 4:23-25, Matthew summarizes the nature of Jesus' ministry throughout Galilee as proclamation and healing, and this combination is continued throughout the Gospel. Immediately following the Sermon on the Mount in Matthew 5–7 (proclamation), Matthew reports a series of miracles concerned with healing (Matt 8–9) as Matthew depicts Jesus as one who makes available the presence and power of God's kingdom to those dwelling on the margins of society in Galilee— a leper, the slave of a Gentile army officer, an old woman, the demon-possessed, a paralytic, a collector of tolls, a young girl, and the blind.

Wesley lived in an age of exciting, unprecedented scientific discovery, when all sorts of mysteries had begun to be explained in terms of natural causes. So he was aware that some educated people had begun to question Jesus' miracles. For example, in his note on Jesus' commission to the disciples that they should "cast out devils" (10:8 AV), Wesley observed that someone had said that diseases ascribed to the devil in the Gospels "have the very same symptoms with the natural diseases of lunacy, epilepsy, or convulsions," leading to the conclusion "that the devil had no hand in them." Wesley continues:

> But it were well to stop and consider a little. Suppose God should allow an evil spirit to usurp the same power over a man's body as the man himself has naturally, and suppose him actually to exercise that power; could we conclude the devil had no hand therein, because his body was bent in the very same manner wherein the man himself bent it naturally?
>
> And suppose God gives an evil spirit a greater power to affect immediately the origin of the nerves in the brain, by irritating them to produce violent motions, or so relaxing them that they can produce little or no motion, still the symptoms will be those of over-tense nerves, as in madness, epilepsies, convulsions, or of relaxed nerves, as in paralytic cases. But could we conclude thence, that the devil had no hand in them?[5]

Reading Wesley's comments, we might forget that serious study of the central nervous system and its relationship to human behavior was barely a century old. Nevertheless, elsewhere Wesley writes that, "for six or seven and twenty years, I had made anatomy and physic the diversion of my leisure hours."[6] In this way, he documented for us his interest in the new worlds that science had begun to open and his desire to take seriously the importance of science for biblical interpretation and for Christian mission. Methodists have always emphasized health care, especially for the poor—and this emphasis goes right back to the health clinics Wesley set up in the eighteenth century. In terms of biblical interpretation, here his solution is openness to the truth of both faith and science; rather than deny the truth of stories of demonized persons in the Gospels or of scientific explanations, he allows that both could be true.

The Gospel of Matthew and Wesley's Concern with Discipleship

The importance of Matthew's Gospel for Wesley is suggested by the number of sermons he drew from it:

- Sermons 21–33: Upon Our Lord's Sermon on the Mount (13 discourses on Matt 5–7)
- Sermon 49: The Cure of Evil-speaking (Matt 18:15-18)
- Sermon 66: The Signs of the Times (Matt 16:3)
- Sermon 84: The Important Question (Matt 16:26)
- Sermon 98: On Visiting the Sick (Matt 25:36)
- Sermon 99: The Reward of Righteousness (Matt 25:34)
- Sermon 108: On Riches (Matt 19:24)
- Sermon 125: On a Single Eye (Matt 6:22-23)
- Sermon 127: On the Wedding Garment (Matt 22:12)
- Sermon 134: Seek First the Kingdom (Matt 6:33)
- Sermon 145: (a sermon outline) In Earth as in Heaven (Matt 6:10)

Notice how many of these—sixteen!—are drawn from the Sermon on the Mount (Matt 5–7). To these may be added several others that, together with his study notes on Matthew's Gospel, make plain Wesley's special interest in Matthew's portrait of holy living.

One of the areas where Wesley's notes invite Christian reflection is *prayer*. His comments have little relationship to workbooks and seminars on prayer on offer today, with their focus on various "technologies" of prayer (different kinds of prayer, things for which to pray, times to pray, prayer-records to keep, postures for praying, etc.). Instead, Wesley's emphasis falls on the One to whom we pray. Speaking of the prayer Jesus taught his disciples in 6:9-13, what we call the "Lord's Prayer," he writes:

> He who best knew what we ought to pray for, and how we ought to pray, what matter of desire, what manner of address, would

most please himself, would best become us, has here dictated to us a most perfect and universal form of prayer, comprehending all our real wants, expressing all our lawful desires—a complete directory and full exercise of all our devotions.[7]

The Lord's Prayer itself he divides into three parts—the preface, the petition, and the conclusion—and he insists that every part is directed to the triune God—Father, Son, and Spirit—and that each section emphasizes the nature of the God to whom we pray. Recognizing God's majesty and mercy, not only do we have all the motivation we need to pray, but we are able to pray from our hearts.

A second area where Matthew's message is especially challenging has to do with *faith and wealth,* a point on which Wesley's rhetoric was unrelenting. In his sermon "On Riches," Wesley reflects on the story of the rich young man in 19:16-30. Wesley:

- Refuses any suggestion that Jesus softens his tough saying about the wealthy: "Truly I tell you, it will be hard for a rich person to enter the kingdom of heaven. Again I tell you, it is easier for a camel to go through the eye of a needle than for someone who is rich to enter the kingdom of God" (19:23-24). Jesus really did mean to say that those who have wealth cannot but place their trust in things.
- Keeps a low bar on what it means to be rich. Anyone is rich who "possesses more than the necessaries and conveniences of life." But what is necessary and "convenient"? He goes on to rule that "whoever has food and raiment sufficient for themselves and their family, *and something over,* is rich" (§4). By this definition, many of us who regard ourselves as "just getting by" or even as "poor" need to look again at Jesus' challenge to the rich.

Why is wealth detrimental to Christian life? Riches are an obstruction to faith; to loving God and neighbor; and to the cultivation of humility, meekness, graciousness, and patience. Wesley refers to these latter qualities as "tempers," a word that we no longer use in this way. We might better think of patterns of believing, thinking, feeling, and behaving that so fully guide our lives that they seem to be inborn qualities. Riches, Wesley urges, distract us from cultivating these patterns. What is more, riches encourage the development of alternative patterns, unholy ones, such as forgetting God (Wesley calls this "atheism"); worshiping things as though they were gods and seeking happiness in things ("idolatry"); taking pride in what we have, as though one's wealth was an index of one's goodness; and a slew of other qualities: self-will, resentment, vengefulness, anxiety, and more.

"Let us come to the point!" we can almost hear Wesley say.

> How many rich people are there among the Methodists (observe, there was not one when they were first joined together!) who actually do "deny themselves, and take up their cross daily"? Who resolutely abstain from every pleasure, either of sense or imagination, unless they know by experience that it prepares them for taking pleasure in God? Who declines no cross, no labor or pain, which lies in the way of one's duty? Who of you that are now rich deny yourselves just as you did when you were poor? Who as willingly endure labor or pain now as you did when you were not worth five pounds? Come to particulars. Do you fast now as often as you did then? Do you rise as early in the morning? Do you endure cold or heat, wind or rain, as cheerfully as ever? See one reason among many why so few increase in goods without decreasing in grace—because they no longer deny themselves and take up their daily cross! They no longer, alas! endure hardship, as good soldiers of Jesus Christ! (§10)

The barometer Wesley gives his Methodists is a hard one. Has the fervor of one's devotion to God and concern for the needs of others changed as a result of increased income?

A third aspect of Wesley's emphasis on discipleship in Matthew's Gospel focuses squarely on Matthew 18 and its counsel regarding *"giving offence"* and *"evil-speaking" within the church.* In his sermon "The Cure of Evil-speaking," Wesley reflects on Jesus' words in Matthew 18:15-17:

> If another member of the church sins against you, go and point out the fault when the two of you are alone. If the member listens to you, you have regained that one. But if you are not

listened to, take one or two others along with you, so that every word may be confirmed by the evidence of two or three witnesses. If the member refuses to listen to them, tell it to the church; and if the offender refuses to listen even to the church, let such a one be to you as a Gentile and a tax collector.

Rather than interpreting this text from within the Gospel of Matthew, as we might expect of preachers today, he sets the stage with words borrowed from Titus 3:2: "Speak evil of no one." This approach carries with it an important assumption, that the individual intentions of the writers of the Gospel of Matthew and the letter to Titus are not the only guide to the meaning of these texts. Wesley does not ask, "I wonder what the author was thinking?" Instead, he operates with the assumption that behind both texts— even though they come from different pens and address different circumstances—stands a single Author. These are the words of God, and from this perspective it makes good sense to ask how one text might illuminate another.

For Wesley, speaking evil of one another cannot be reduced to lying or slandering. He thinks more along the lines of today's category of "gossip":

> For evil-speaking is neither more nor less than speaking evil of an absent person; relating something evil that was really done or said by one that is not present when it is related. Suppose, having seen someone drunk, or heard someone curse or swear, I tell this when that person is absent, it is evil-speaking. In our language this is also by an extremely proper name termed "backbiting." Nor is there any material difference between this and what we usually style "talebearing." If the tale be delivered in a soft and quiet manner (perhaps with expressions of good-will to the person, and of hope that things may not be quite so bad) then we call it "whispering." But in whatever manner it be done the thing is the same—the same in substance if not in circumstance. Still it is evil-speaking. (§1)

Wesley must not have known the practice so widespread among Christians today—of sharing "prayer concerns" as a way of trafficking in scuttlebutt; otherwise, he surely would have condemned this, too, as "evil-speaking."

Although Wesley elaborates at length on the procedures set out in Matthew 18, the basic guard against evil-speaking is straightforward: Talk to the person who committed the offense (with its corollary: Do not talk to others about the person who committed the offense). "Can anything be plainer?" Wesley asks.[8]

Wesley devotes a sermon to this text, as well as a couple of pages in his *Explanatory Notes upon the New Testament*. I mention this because, clearly, he did not latch onto every passage in Scripture the way he did this one. What propelled this text off the pages of the New Testament and into this kind of attention? Undoubtedly, this is due to the premium Wesley placed on genuine Christian fellowship, which included ingredients like truth-telling and accountability. Indeed, further along in the sermon he writes, "Let this be the distinguishing mark of a Methodist: 'They censure no one behind their backs'" (§III.5). This is how Christians put into practice their love and care for one another.[9]

Finally, there is the issue of *holiness* itself, which Wesley develops in several ways in his reflections on the Gospel of Matthew. For example, he seems to think of the Sermon on the Mount (Matt 5–7) as a tract on holiness. Matthew 5, and especially the Beatitudes, describe "the nature of inward holiness." Matthew 6 "describes that purity of intention without which none of our outward actions are holy." And Matthew 7 "warns us against the chief hindrances of holiness."[10] Even from this outline, we see Wesley's interest in holiness of heart giving rise to holiness of life.

This is demonstrated well in Wesley's sermon "On the Wedding Garment," based on the parable of the royal wedding banquet (22:1-14). This parable has two related concerns: who gets invited to the banquet and who is appropriately attired for it. Wesley's concern is the second half of the parable, in which someone who had been invited and had joined the party was forcefully removed.

> But when the king came in to see the guests, he noticed a man there who was not wearing a wedding robe, and he said to him, "Friend, how did you get in here without a wedding robe?" And he was speechless. Then the king said to the attendants, "Bind him hand and foot, and throw him into the outer darkness, where there will be weeping and gnashing of teeth." For many are called, but few are chosen. (22:11-14)

Here is a puzzle: This man had responded to the royal invitation and, having been invited, he has joined others in the wedding hall, yet his garment indicates that he does not belong. Why? In what way does the man's clothing insult the king? What does he lack by way of outward attire? Wesley responds that what is lacking "is the 'holiness without which no man shall see the Lord'":

> The righteousness of Christ is, doubtless, necessary for any soul that enters into glory. But so is personal holiness, too, for every person. But it is highly needful to be observed that they are necessary in different respects. The former is necessary to entitle us to heaven; the latter, to qualify us for it. Without the righteousness of Christ we could have no claim to glory; without holiness we could have no fitness for it. By the former we become members of Christ, children of God, and heirs of the kingdom of heaven. By the latter we are "made meet to be partakers of the inheritance of the saints in light." (§10)

Here is a hallmark of Wesleyan faith. Becoming Christian is not simply an event in the past; rather, one "becomes" Christian through ongoing formation of heart and life in ways that reflect the image of Christ. It is the renewal of the person "in the image of God wherein it was created." It is "faith that works by love." "It works love to God and all humankind," and it produces in believers such character qualities as "lowliness, meekness, gentleness, temperance, and long-suffering."

> "It is neither circumcision," the attending on all the Christian ordinances, "nor uncircumcision," the fulfilling of all heathen morality, but "the keeping of the commandments of God"; particularly those, "You will love the Lord your God with all your heart, and your neighbor as yourself."

Wesley concludes: "In a word, holiness is the having 'the mind that was in Christ,' and the 'walking as Christ walked'" (§17).

Again, we should notice how Wesley is making sense of the Scriptures. He is not like one of our contemporary Bible scholars concerned primarily with what Jesus thought he was saying or what the Gospel writer intended to communicate by reporting

Jesus' parable, or even what Matthew's first audience might have imagined they heard. Wesley is interpreting Matthew's Gospel according to a theological pattern that takes into account the whole of Scripture. This pattern is the "way of salvation" and it touches important points of the parable of the royal wedding banquet:

- God graciously invites
- People respond negatively or positively to God's gracious initiative
- Those who respond negatively bring judgment upon themselves
- Those who respond positively demonstrate their faith by continuing the journey of salvation through holiness of heart and life.

Rather than simply reading this or that text on its own terms, then, Wesley located biblical texts within the overarching pattern of Scripture. He worked to read biblical texts within the architecture of the overall scriptural message. What is more, he sought for himself and for Methodists everywhere that he and they should be so formed according to this pattern of thought that they would understand not only biblical texts but all of life according to the overall architecture of Scripture.

Questions for Reflection and Discussion

1. If we understand that Jesus is our Messiah, what does it mean for you to say, "Jesus is Lord of my life"?
2. According to Wesley, the kingdom of heaven is the people of God gathered and acting together to do God's will. What would have to happen for your church to become a foretaste of heaven here on earth?
3. What does it mean to say that our first allegiance is to God? What and who takes your first priority?
4. How do you understand the miracles of Jesus? What is the difference between Jesus' miracles and magic? Have you ever seen a miracle?
5. Wesley emphasized the One to whom we pray. Discuss how, when, and where you pray. Does your prayer life bring you into

a deeper fellowship with God? How? Share a meaningful prayer experience.

6. Is wealth detrimental to Christian life? Why is money so hard to talk about in the church?

7. All agree that "evil speaking" and gossip are divisive and hurtful. What can you do to make sure that people can share prayer concerns and personal stories in confidence?

8. Wesley was concerned about holiness of heart and life. Think of persons you know who demonstrate holiness. What are their characteristics? What are some ways that you could become more like Jesus?

2

Gospel of Mark

The first fifteen verses of Mark's Gospel map the coming of Jesus in relation to God's work to bring salvation to God's people. Mark 1:1-15 looks backward and forward in order to identify Jesus and his proclamation of the kingdom of God as the realization of God's promise to deliver Israel. If Mark 1:1-15 is the prologue of the Gospel of Mark, this makes the two scenes of disciple-calling (1:16-20) the first events in the actual narrative Mark has written. This focuses our attention from the outset of Mark's narrative on the big story of God's saving activity *and* on the immediate consequences of God's work for human response, discipleship.

At the turn of the fifth century, Augustine (A.D. 354–430) studied the relationships among the New Testament Gospels and concluded that the Gospel of Matthew was written first and Mark second:

> Mark follows [Matthew] closely, and looks like his assistant and epitomizer.[1] For in his narrative he gives nothing apart from the [other Gospels] that agrees with John. He has little to record distinctly on his own. He has still less in common with Luke that is distinct from the rest. But he has a very great number of passages in common with Matthew. He also narrates much in words almost the same in number and identity as those used by Matthew, where this agreement is either with that evangelist alone, or with him in connection with the rest. (*Harmony of the Gospels* 1.2.4)

This is a nice summary of Gospel relationships, since only twenty-four verses in the Gospel of Mark are unique to Mark. Put differently, more than 95 percent of the material found in Mark's

Gospel is also found in the Gospels of Matthew and Luke. The view that Mark abridged Matthew held sway from the days of the early church through the last half of the eighteenth century.[2] Indeed, John Wesley thought that Mark "presupposes that of St. Matthew, and supplies what is omitted therein": "St. Mark wrote a short compendium, and yet added many remarkable circumstances omitted by St. Matthew, particularly with regard to the apostles, immediately after they were called."[3] Wesley thus participated in the general lack of interest in the Gospel of Mark that persisted for centuries in deference to the Gospel of Matthew.

Since Wesley's day, the Gospel of Mark has been recovered, in part because, from the turn of the nineteenth century on, New Testament scholars have tended to assume that the Gospel of Mark was written first, followed by Matthew and Luke, thus reversing the earlier, standard judgment regarding the chronology of the Gospels. Additionally, the Gospel of Mark was reassessed for its importance as a source for those interested in reconstructing the historical Jesus and because students of the Gospels have recently come to recognize the profundity of its message. Mark's narrative today is sometimes referred to as the Second Gospel not because it was the second to have been written, then, but because it is the second in order among the four Gospels found in the New Testament.

Rehabilitation of the Gospel of Mark postdates Wesley's day, so it is not surprising that his interest in it is diminished in comparison with his work on Matthew. True, among his sermons, six are based on Markan texts:

- Sermon 7: "The Way to the Kingdom" (Mark 1:15)
- Sermon 14: "The Repentance of Believers" (Mark 1:15)
- Sermon 38: "A Caution against Bigotry" (Mark 9:38-39)
- Sermon 73: "Of Hell" (Mark 9:48)
- Sermon 120: "The Unity of the Divine Being" (Mark 12:33)
- Sermon 144: "The Love of God" (Mark 12:30)

However, with the exception of his preaching on the kingdom of God, the others hardly bring into focus central concerns of the Second Gospel. Accordingly, in this chapter I want first to highlight some Markan emphases that are important for Wesleyans interested in reading the Gospel of Mark theologically today. Afterward, I will turn to Wesley's interest in Mark 1:15 and, finally, to his sermon on Mark 9:38-39, "A Caution against Bigotry."

Mark's Gospel: A Biography of Jesus

One important way to begin reading a book is to ask, What is it? We expect certain things from novels, we have different expectations of newspaper articles, and we look for still other things when we pick up a theology textbook. What should we expect of the book Mark has written? What kind of book is it? Although we think of Mark's book as a "gospel," the prior question is what it would have looked like to the Evangelist and to his early readers. Actually, Mark's narrative conforms most closely to the genre of biography, a form of Greco-Roman literature that grew out of the practice of history-writing as particular persons became the focus of study and writing. Thinking of Mark as a biography helps to explain why it proceeds along roughly chronological lines, from the appearance of Jesus in Galilee to his final journey to Jerusalem.

Of course, Mark's book differs from contemporary biographies we might have on our bookshelves. Psychological motivations, childhood influences, physical appearance, date of birth—we expect this sort of information from today's writers, but these played little or no role in the Roman world of Mark's day. In antiquity a biography related the significance of famous people's careers, rarely focusing on their childhoods but often including reference to the way they died (for how people died was regarded as a measure of their character). What is more, "famous" people did not achieve their fame by standing out from the crowd but rather by embodying the qualities valued by society-at-large or by one of its subsets. Mark's Gospel would have been written, then, for Christian communities who admired already and had begun to adopt the unconventional values proclaimed and lived by Jesus.

Who is Jesus? This question is front and center. It breaks out into the open in 8:27, 29, where Jesus asks of his disciples, in turn,

"Who do people say that I am?" and "Who do you say that I am?" However, the questions begin much earlier. The crowds ask of one another, "What is this? A new teaching—with authority!" (1:27). Demons do not ask, but seem to perceive already who Jesus is: "I know who you are, the Holy One of God!" (1:24); "What have you to do with me, Jesus, Son of the Most High God?" (5:7; cf. 1:34). Jesus' opponents worry over his identity, too, wondering about the basis of his authority: "Where did this man get all this? What is this wisdom that has been given to him?" (6:2). "By what authority are you doing these things?" (11:28; see also 2:7, 16, 24; 3:21-22; 6:14-16).

God, on the other hand, is clear about Jesus' identity. Twice God claims Jesus as "my Son, the beloved" (1:11; 9:7), and Jesus affirms this relationship in his Gethsemane prayer: "Abba, Father" (14:36; see also 13:32). When he is asked by the high priest at his trial before the Jewish Council, "Are you the Messiah, the Son of the Blessed One?" Jesus replies, "I am" (14:61-62). This perspective is also shared by Mark the Evangelist (1:1) and by the centurion at the cross: "Truly this man was God's Son!" (15:39).

Perhaps most puzzling to us, and frustrating to Jesus, is the failure of Jesus' own disciples to comprehend his identity. After hearing him teach and watching him work miracles, even after they had received private instruction (e.g., 4:34) and "been given the secret of the kingdom of God" (4:11), they are stunned by his mastery of the storm and sea: "Who then is this, that even the wind and the sea obey him?" (4:41). When he comes to them walking on the sea, they take him for a ghost (6:49). If his teaching and miracles are not the key to what Jesus is about, what is?

Mark's Gospel: It Is about God

Mark's Gospel is a biography of Jesus, but for Mark this is almost secondary. His real interest is not focused on giving us some interesting details about Jesus' life. Jesus is more than the titles given him, and more than his healing and teaching. Rather than give us a list of titles and actions, then, Mark gives us a "storied" picture of Jesus. He weaves a narrative that will help us grasp Jesus' significance, and his weaving includes not only reports about Jesus but also colorful threads taken from the Old Testament. In this way, Mark frames his presentation of the mission of Jesus as a story first and foremost about the God of Israel now present to set things right. If we are caught up in the narrative Mark tells, we ourselves may be transformed by Jesus' call to a discipleship that requires that we give up everything so as to live lives determined by the life of Jesus.

This becomes clear in the opening verses of the Gospel. My translation will depart from the NRSV in order to make plain that the beginning of the gospel lies not with John the Baptist nor even with Jesus. It has its roots in divine promise of liberation of Israel from the bondage of exile related by the prophet Isaiah, particularly in Isaiah 40:

> The beginning of the good news of Jesus Christ, Son of God, happened just as it was written about in Isaiah's prophecy: "Look, I am sending my messenger before you who will prepare your way; a voice shouting in the wilderness: 'Prepare the way of the Lord; make his paths straight.'" (Mark 1:1-3, my translation)

In other words, Mark informs his audience that, if they want to understand the significance of Jesus, they need to read Isaiah. If they want to grasp the meaning of the gospel Jesus proclaims and enacts in his miracles, they need to situate Jesus in the story of restoration Isaiah had anticipated. Or, better, they need to read Jesus' mission as the fulfillment of God's promise to restore Israel from exile.

The grand story within which Mark locates the life, death, and resurrection of Jesus, then, is not the story of an individual person today mired in sin and needing rescue. It is much bigger than this. With the coming of Jesus, God is on the move in the world he has made to gather his people, Jew and Gentile, and to establish his reign in their hearts and lives as the community that worships God and embodies God's character, and that invites others to do the same. The coming of Jesus is good news for individuals today who are mired in sin and needing rescue because God's kingdom repeals all other kingdoms, including the reign of sin in human lives and those overbearing powers that keep folks from embracing and living lives freed for love of God and love of neighbor.

Building on the ground of Isaiah's expectation, Mark gives us a good idea of what he means by "good news" or "gospel." For the Romans, "good news" might be the message brought from the battlefield, announcing Roman victory, or words that celebrate and honor Rome's emperor. With Isaiah in the background, though, Mark takes a different path in his understanding of "gospel." Longing for the age of promise, the Isaianic herald speaks of the "good news" as the coming of God (40:9), the saving reign of God in peace and justice (52:7), the work of God on behalf of the outcast (61:1-2). Here are Israel's hopes for divine intervention and rule, and for the restoration of God's people. Clearly, then, the sovereign rule of God is defined in opposition to the sovereign rule of Rome. Authentic peace, the promised good news of God, does not come through the subjugation of people but through their release by God, and through the restoration of God's people under God's banner of salvation.

In short, the story of Jesus is the story of God's purpose for our planet coming to fruition. Accordingly, Mark can summarize the mission and message of Jesus with these words found at the close of the Gospel's prologue:

> Jesus came into Galilee announcing God's good news:
> > The long-awaited time has come!
> > God's kingdom is upon us!
> > Repent and believe the good news! (1:14b-15, my translation)

The story of Jesus is thus the story of fulfillment, the story of God's new exodus. We hear echoes of the exodus story everywhere—feeding the thousands in the wilderness, crossing the sea, mastery of the sea, journeying throughout Galilee, the episode on the Mount of Transfiguration. These events find their meaning in the past, to be sure, but also in the present as they anticipate the future of God's kingdom fully realized. Everything—Jesus' teaching, his healing, his exorcisms—puts on display the good news that God's kingdom is upon us and is thus grounded in Mark's portrait of God's intervention to restore God's people. Even Jesus' death, which casts its shadow across the whole of Mark's Gospel, is the means by which God liberates God's people (10:45).

Mark's Gospel thus bears witness to the changing of the ages. If the long-awaited time has come and the kingdom of God is upon us, this calls for living lives in keeping with the new era Jesus' coming has inaugurated. At the beginning of the prologue, Mark borrows words from Isaiah 40:3 as a call for human response: "Prepare the way of the Lord; make his paths straight." The prologue ends with urgent words, "Repent, and believe in the good news!" To paraphrase this summary of Jesus' preaching, we might say that he urges people *to declare their ultimate allegiance* to God, *to discern* what God is doing, *to realign their lives* in relation to what God is doing, and *to step out in lives of discipleship* characterized by God's saving agenda.

In Jesus, God keeps his promises and inaugurates God's reign and rule, his kingdom. Jesus' mission—including his life, death, and the empty tomb—calls for and enables human response to God that Mark develops in terms of Christlike discipleship. In an ultimate sense, then, the Gospel of Mark is about God.

John Wesley and Mark 1:15

This sketch of the message of the Second Gospel leans heavily on the opening verses of Mark. This is not accidental, but neither is it a pragmatic choice. Like the opening of any book, Mark's prologue provides a lens by which to view the rest. Already we have an affirmation of some important Wesleyan motifs—even if Wesley himself did not develop his understanding of the Gospel of Mark in quite this way. Let me give a couple of examples. First, as in Wesleyan thought more generally, so here it is clear that the call for human faith and action is grounded in the prior, enabling work of God. As Wesley writes in another context, "For, first, God works; therefore you *can* work. Secondly, God works; therefore you *must* work."[4] Second, Mark's Gospel is read in relation to other biblical texts—in this case, especially the prophet Isaiah. Here, we have turned to Isaiah because we have been invited to do so by the Second Evangelist (Mark 1:1-3), and so we see that Scripture can be understood to tell the one story of God's work to fulfill God's mission.

Wesley marked the importance of Mark 1:15 by turning to it

twice in his sermons. The first is his sermon "The Way to the Kingdom." The first half of the sermon focuses on the nature of the kingdom. Surprisingly for us, Wesley's thinking about the kingdom in this context is drawn not from the words of Jesus in Mark's Gospel but from Paul's words in Romans 14:17: "For the kingdom of God is not food and drink but righteousness and peace and joy in the Holy Spirit." This is a reminder that Wesley presupposes that the many and diverse books of the Bible evidence nonetheless a single voice, the voice of God. Hence, he is willing to find synergy in putting otherwise disparate texts next to each other, since both refer to the kingdom of God. This may seem strange to us if we have learned the mantra of modern biblical study: Context, context, context.... But in Wesley's defense, we should observe that none of the Gospels actually ever *define* "kingdom of God," whereas Paul seems to do just that in Romans 14.

Turning to Paul's words in the Letter to the Romans, Wesley takes "food and drink" as a reference to "outward things," like ceremonies, rituals, and forms of worship (§I.2-5). "True religion" (which, Wesley urges, is only another way of saying "kingdom of God") does not reside in right actions of any kind, nor even in right doctrine. This is because neither *orthodoxy* ("right doctrine") nor *orthopraxy* ("right action") can substitute for *orthokardia* ("right heart").

This emphasis is as important as it is difficult to grasp, since Wesley was committed to both right doctrine and right behavior, both for himself and for all Methodists. For example, in his pamphlet "The Character of a Methodist," he writes that

> the distinguishing marks of Methodists are not their opinions of any sort. Their assenting to this or that scheme of religion, their embracing any particular set of notions, their espousing the judgment of one person or of another, are all quite wide of the point.... We believe, indeed, that "all Scripture is given by the inspiration of God."... We believe the written word of God to be the only and sufficient rule both of Christian faith and practice.... We believe Christ to be the eternal, supreme God. (§1)

In other words, when it comes to doctrine, Methodists affirm the faith of the Christian church as this is set forth in the creeds. Wesley goes on:

Nor do we desire to be distinguished by actions, customs, or usages, of an indifferent nature.... It does not lie in the form of our apparel, in the posture of our body, or the covering of our heads; nor yet in abstaining from marriage, or from meats and drinks, which are all good if received with thanksgiving. Therefore, neither will anyone... fix the mark of a Methodist here, in any actions or customs purely indifferent, undetermined by the word of God. (§3)

Wesley then asks, "What then is the mark? I answer: Methodist are those who have 'the love of God shed abroad in their hearts by the Holy Spirit...'; those who 'love the Lord their God with all their heart, and with all their soul, and with all their mind, and with all their strength'" (§5).

Wesley makes just this point in his sermon, "The Way to the Kingdom":

Someone may be orthodox in every point; they may not only espouse right opinions, but zealously defend them against all opposers; they may think justly concerning the incarnation of our Lord, concerning the ever blessed Trinity, and every other doctrine contained in the oracles of God. They may assent to all the three creeds—that called the Apostles', the Nicene, and the Athanasian—and yet it is possible that they may have no religion at all.... They may be almost as orthodox as the devil... and may all the while be as great a stranger as the devil to the religion of the heart. (§I.6)

Wesley thus draws from Paul's words this emphasis on the inner life, the heart, where righteousness, peace, and joy in the Holy Spirit take up lodging. This is a matter of emphasis, though, since, in fact, right belief, right action, and right heart comprise an inseparable triumvirate. "A threefold cord is not quickly broken" (Eccl 4:12).

The second half of Wesley's sermon addresses the question, How might we enter into the kingdom? This is an important question not only because it introduces how Wesley goes on to interpret Mark 1:15 but also because the way Wesley phrases the question actually stands in tension with the way he has thus far interpreted the kingdom. Having explained the kingdom of God above all in terms of the inner life of the believer, he leaves little room for the imagery of the kingdom as something *into which we enter*. This is because the kingdom of God seems to be "within us" rather than our being within it.[5]

Wesley has unfortunately followed a mistranslation of Luke 17:21 in his English Bible, the Authorized (or King James) Version of 1711. In dialogue with the Pharisees over when the kingdom of God would come, Jesus there observes that people will not have to look here or there for the kingdom since the kingdom of God— now following the Greek text—*entos hymōn estin*. The AV translates, "The kingdom of God *is within you*" (emphasis added). This is a troublesome translation not only because it misrepresents the use of the Greek term *entos*, but also because it makes Jesus say that his opponents possess the kingdom of God. Undoubtedly, Wesley would never have agreed that the Pharisees who oppose Jesus are characterized by the true religion of the heart! To the contrary, Jesus in Luke's Gospel is claiming that the kingdom of God "is among you" (NRSV) or "is in your midst" (NASB).[6] In fact, the kingdom of God is "among" even these Pharisees because Jesus himself makes present God's kingdom.

Already in his work on Romans 14 in the first half of his sermon, Wesley might have recognized the importance of the kingdom not only for the heart but also for the social order among those who live out their allegiance to God. What was at issue in Roman congregations were eating habits that divided believers from one another. Paul declares that these matters are irrelevant on account of believers' overriding commitment to the rule of God. Righteousness, peace, and joy, not fussing and separating over food or drink, characterize Christian congregations made alive by the Spirit of God. Similarly, in Mark 1:15, Jesus' reference to the kingdom of God emphasizes God's activity in the whole world, including but not limited to the hearts of believers. Jesus' teaching leads to forms of discipleship exemplified by Simon and Andrew, James and John, who left everything, including economic and family ties, to follow Jesus. (Here we see "right heart" bundled together with "right behavior.")

Of course, this broader perspective on the kingdom of God is not alien to Wesley, even if he does not develop it here. His comments on Matt 3:2 interpret God's kingdom in terms of the present state of life among the subjects of God's kingdom.[7] This means two things:

1. Even if Wesley justifiably prioritizes a right heart (*orthokardia*), this can never really be separated from right doctrine (*orthodoxy*) and right behavior (*orthopraxy*).
2. Jesus' teaching about the kingdom of God concerns our perception of the whole work of God in the world, together with the call we have to participate in the whole of what God is doing in the world.

Actually, these are two ways of saying the same thing, since Jesus' proclamation of the kingdom calls to us for change in our beliefs, thoughts, feelings, and behaviors. Nothing can be the same.

The second half of Wesley's sermon "The Way to the Kingdom" is concerned, then, with how one might enter into the kingdom. Following the logic of Jesus' proclamation, Wesley gives two answers. First, repent—that is, "Know yourself to be a sinner, and what manner of sinner you are" (§II.1). Here Wesley goes to some length to disrobe any pretensions to human goodness, to map the distance between God and sinful humanity, and thus to show sinners their true situation. The second response follows from the first: "One step more and you will enter in. You 'repent.' Now, 'believe the gospel'" (§II.7). Just as Wesley had gone into some graphic detail regarding the sin that overpowered our lives and thus the necessity of repentance, so now he details the nature of the gospel. For him, the "gospel" is "the whole revelation made to people by Jesus" (§II.8), summarized in texts like John 3:16: "For God so loved the world that he gave his only Son, so that everyone who believes in him may not perish but may have eternal life"; or 1 Timothy 1:15: "Christ Jesus came into the world to save sinners."

Wesley is not finished with Mark 1:15. If repentance is the means by which people enter the kingdom, what about those who have entered the kingdom and do not yet live fully according to its ways? For help, Wesley borrows language from the New Testament book of Hebrews in order to highlight the portrait of discipleship as moving along on a journey toward greater and

25

greater faithfulness. The idea of discipleship as a journey is very much at home in the Gospel of Mark, too. Already in its opening verses, we hear the voice in the wilderness, "Prepare *the way* of the Lord; make *his paths* straight" (1:3, emphasis added), and the terminology of travel and roads (or "the way") dots the landscape of Mark's narrative.[8] "The way" is sometimes a means by which Mark connects his story with the wilderness wanderings of Israel in the exodus story and sometimes a way to trace the formation of discipleship. Thinking of discipleship as a journey reminds us that our dispositions, commitments, attitudes, and character are not changed overnight but require ongoing (trans)formation.

Wesley thus taught that repentance must be understood in two ways. The first is a conviction of sin that leads to faith and justification. The second refers to change of heart and life after justification. Here, too, repentance and faith go hand in hand.

> By repentance we feel the sin remaining in our hearts, and cleaving to our words and actions. By faith we receive the power of God in Christ, purifying our hearts and cleansing our hands. By repentance we are still sensible that we deserve punishment for all our tempers and words and actions. By faith we are conscious that our advocate with the Father is continually pleading for us, and thereby continually turning aside all condemnation and punishment from us. By repentance we have an abiding conviction that there is no help in us. By faith we receive not only mercy, but "grace to help in every time of need." Repentance disclaims the very possibility of any other help. Faith accepts all the help we stand in need of from him that has all power in heaven and earth. Repentance says, "Without him I can do nothing"; faith says, "I can do all things through Christ strengthening me." (§II.6)

Wesley and "Bigotry"

The last example of Wesley's work with the Second Gospel is his sermon "A Caution against Bigotry," based on Mark 9:38-39:

> John said to him, "Teacher, we saw someone casting out demons in your name, and we tried to stop him, because he was not following us." But Jesus said, "Do not stop him; for no one who

does a deed of power in my name will be able soon afterward to speak evil of me."

I tend to think of "bigotry" as the rough equivalent of "prejudice," but in the eighteenth century its sense was more specific: a narrow, partisan attitude intolerant of those outside one's group. By speaking against bigotry, then, Wesley developed for his readers a keen sense of the openhandedness toward other Christians, believers and groups of believers, which ought to characterize Methodists.

What we must not miss about the issue John raises is John's last word, *us*. John, one of the twelve apostles, does not charge this unnamed exorcist with not following Jesus. Rather, he says that this man was not following "us." What an irony: John and his fellow apostles had taken it upon themselves to draw the circle around who could or could not be regarded as a Jesus-follower, taking as the basis of their judgment something other than following Jesus!

Wesley's approach to the matter is to spend considerable energy explaining what "casting out demons" means in our world. He takes a very different path than Hollywood. He does not concern himself with how to identify a demonized person, he does not discuss the liturgies by which demons are thrown out of a person, and he does not warn of the arduous nature of doing battle with the devil's minions. Instead, he observes that, as the Holy Spirit is at work in the lives of believers, so the devil is at work in the lives of those who are not yet followers of Jesus.

> He blinds the eyes of their understanding so that the light of the glorious gospel of Christ cannot shine upon them. He chains their souls down to earth and hell with the chains of their own vile affections. He binds them down to the earth by love of the world, love of money, of pleasure, of praise. And by pride, envy, anger, hate, revenge, he causes their souls to draw nigh unto hell; acting the more secure and uncontrolled because they know not that he acts at all. (§I.6)

Casting out demons, then, is nothing more or less than the work of evangelism, bringing people to repentance and faith in

Christ—that is, the gospel-centered work of all believers, whether lay or clergy. Wesley concludes this section of his sermon by underscoring a key point: "All this is indeed the work of God. It is God alone who can cast out Satan" (§I.14). If this is true, how could someone engaged in the work of overturning the rule of evil be anything other than a follower of Christ?

This leads to the question of what it might mean for this evangelist not to be a follower of "us." Wesley takes us through a list of possibilities (§II):

- We don't know who this evangelist is.
- This evangelist is not a member of our band of believers.
- This evangelist does not share some of our "religious opinions" concerning things that are not central to Christian doctrine.[9]
- This evangelist may be more at home with practices of worship associated with a Calvin or a Luther than a Methodist.

Although Wesley considers other possibilities, he denies that this person has any material differences with the apostles. The bottom line is that those involved in bringing people to repentance and faith can only be "one of us," even if they do not "follow us." Anyone who stands in the way of such people is guilty of bigotry, so "strong an attachment to, or fondness for, our own party, opinion, Church, and religion" that we fail to identify those who work against the rule of evil and in concert with God's Spirit as anything but God's people. Therefore, Wesley urges, "Neither directly nor indirectly discourage or hinder anyone who brings sinners from the power of Satan to God, 'because he was not following us,' in opinions, modes of worship, or anything else which does not affect the essence of religion."[10] Here is a profound statement about the character of Christian unity.[11]

Questions for Reflection and Discussion

1. Does understanding the Gospel of Mark as a biography of Jesus change how you read it? How does this biography compare with others you have read?

2. People heard Jesus speak with authority. Today, we might say that Jesus had the credentials to speak with authority. What does it mean to say that someone is an authority or has authority on a given topic or subject? Think of some people you respect. What kind of authority do they have?

3. What credentials and authority do you have?

4. The Gospel of Mark suggests that through Jesus, God was on the move in this world. Where do you see God working in your world today? in your church? in your family?

5. There is an old camp song titled "His Banner over Me Is Love." God promises to seek us so that we can be in a right relationship with God and with each other. If God placed a banner over your home, what would it say? If God placed a banner over your church to describe its witness, what would it say?

6. John Wesley read each part of Scripture as an aspect of the whole of Scripture. This was a guiding principle in his interpretation and understanding of particular biblical passages. What might that say about Wesley's knowledge of the Bible? Do you feel confident in your knowledge of the whole tenor of Scripture? How might you improve?

7. Wesley believed that a warm heart should lead to active participation in mission and ministry. Looking at your faith community and Christian fellowships, where do you need to be more active in service?

3
Gospel of Luke

We turn to the Gospel of Luke for some of our most loved and in-
fluential of Jesus' parables, including the prodigal son (15:11-32)
and the good Samaritan (10:25-37), both of which appear only in
Luke's narrative. Luke's Gospel is sometimes called the Third
Gospel because of its position after the Gospels of Mark and
Matthew. And if we set it side by side with these other two, the
Third Gospel is perhaps most remarkable for its unrelenting interest in the marginalized and dispossessed, its lengthy story of
the birth of Jesus (chaps. 1–2), and the long "travel account" that
occupies the central section of the Gospel (9:51–19:48). We learn
quickly that, in Lukan thought, salvation is focused on the topsy-
turvy work of God, who, in the words of Mary, "has shown
strength with his arm" and "has scattered the proud in the
thoughts of their hearts" (1:51). She goes on to say, "He has
brought down the powerful from their thrones, and lifted up the
lowly; he has filled the hungry with good things, and sent the rich
away empty" (1:52-53).

We also learn that Jesus is on a journey, and those who would
follow him in discipleship sign up for a lengthy journey, the journey of salvation, which, itself, is a journey of transformation.

As Wesley recognized, another remarkable feature of the
Gospel of Luke is the special relationship it shares with the Acts
of the Apostles. A comparison of their respective prefaces, both of
which contain dedications to Theophilus (Luke 1:1-4; Acts 1:1-2),
demonstrate that the Acts of the Apostles is a continuation of
the narrative begun in the Third Gospel.[1] Luke was alone among
the Evangelists in regarding the story of Jesus as somehow

incomplete without showing its continuation in the life of the community and mission begun in Jesus' ministry.

The Message of the Gospel of Luke

The message of Luke's Gospel is concerned above all with the theme of salvation—its derivation, scope, and embodiment. Not surprisingly, then, the Gospel of Luke is centered on God. Even if God makes few direct appearances in the Gospel, God's agenda drives the story forward. God is introduced as "my Savior" (1:47), and God reveals his purpose in a variety of ways—through the Scriptures, through heavenly messengers, through the Holy Spirit, through his own voice, through the divine choreography of events, and through those who speak on God's behalf, most notably Jesus of Nazareth.

God's will is set in motion through the Spirit-anointed ministry of Jesus (3:21-22; 4:18-19). His teaching and healing mark God's priorities and invite others to get in sync with God's work in the world. Jesus is portrayed as a prophet, but more than a prophet. He is the long-awaited Messiah, Son of David, Son of God, who fulfills his career as a regal prophet for whom death, while necessary, is not the last word. For Jesus' disciples, the struggle is not so much to discern *who* Jesus is, but how he can be the Messiah *and* undergo humiliation and death. How can Jesus be God's "anointed one" (for this is what "Messiah" means) *and* be rejected by people?

Early on, Jesus is identified as savior (2:11), and this is the role he fulfills in numerous ways. Among the most visible are his miracles of healing and exorcism, together with the character of his table fellowship. The miracles Jesus performs and the people with whom he shares meals both embody the truth of the inbreaking kingdom of God. They demonstrate that Jesus reads the progression of time in reverse: Because God's future is breaking into the present, so the future realization of God's purpose determines present-day commitments and practices. Jesus heals those who, on account of their maladies, live on the margins of their communities. His table companions are not carefully chosen so as to parade Jesus' prestige in the wider world; instead, he eats with toll collectors and sinners (e.g., 15:1-2). Through these avenues, Jesus communicates the presence of divine salvation for those who dwell on the periphery of acceptable society.

In fact, it is not too much to say that, for Luke, discipleship entails "friendship" with the marginal people of this world. This is congruent with his inaugural proclamation:

> The Spirit of the Lord is upon me!
> He has anointed me!
> He has sent me to proclaim good news to outcasts! (4:18, my translation)

Why do I translate the Greek term *ptōchos* as "outcast," rather than "poor," as with most translations (for example, NIV, NRSV)? This is because today we tend to understand the word *poor* as a reference to money, and folks in the first century had a wider view of things. If we think about it, we can see that "poor" often includes more than money for us, too. In any case, to be "poor" or "outcast" or "marginal" might be defined in a number of ways in the first-century world of Luke's Gospel. Relative wealth would certainly be included, though other factors would count, too. This is because, in the Roman world, barometers of "belonging" and "prestige" included money, but also health and religious purity, parentage and sex, occupation and education, to name a few.[2]

In important ways, Jesus' habits of ministry put on display his teaching. Jesus' instruction is often striking for its emphasis on a particular vision of God and the sort of world order that might reflect this vision of God. Throughout the Gospel, but especially in the story of Jesus' journey with his disciples from Galilee to Jerusalem (9:51–19:48), Jesus attempts to transform the view of God held by his followers. He wants them to recognize and embrace fully God as their Father, the God whose desire is to embrace them with gracious care and provision (e.g., 11:1-13; 12:32). Jesus shapes his followers at the deepest levels so that they might serve the kingdom of God.

In an important sense, then, this narrative about God is concerned with the formation of the people of God, who will later be known as the people of "the Way,"[3] the church. Luke writes a

Gospel that, in the end, concerns itself with the history, beliefs, and practices that define the community of God's people, and with the invitation to participate in God's redemptive project.

The call to discipleship in Luke is at a basic level an invitation for persons to align themselves with Jesus' mission and, thus, with the purpose of God. Inclusion in the community of God's people is no longer centered on ancestral heritage. "Bear fruits worthy of repentance," John the Baptist announces. "Do not begin to say to yourselves, 'We have Abraham as our ancestor'; for I tell you, God is able from these stones to raise up children to Abraham" (3:8). Now the focus is on lives that reflect God's own priorities, God's own character. Genuine "children of Abraham" produce "fruits in keeping with repentance." Jesus' family consists of "those who hear the word of God and do it" (8:21). This involves openhanded mercy to those in need.

Jesus calls people to live as he lives, in contrast to ways of life typical of the larger Roman world. Do good to those who hate you. Extend hospitality to those who cannot return the favor. Give without expectation of return. Such behaviors grow out of service in the kingdom of God. They are possible only for those whose convictions and commitments have been transformed by the goodness of God. For Luke's Gospel, the primary competitor for this focus is Wealth—not so much money itself, but the rule of Money, expressed in human hunger for social praise and in lives divorced from the least, the lost, and the left out.

It almost goes without saying, then, that, from the first page to the last, Luke's Gospel is concerned with a salvation that embraces everyday life lived in the present. That is, salvation includes but can never be limited to only spiritual or future matters. Salvation signals the restoration of the integrity of human life and the commissioning of the community of God's people to put God's grace into practice among themselves and within ever-widening circles of outsiders.

Wesley and the Gospel of Luke

Given this brief overview of some of Luke's central emphases, we should not be surprised to learn that Wesley was especially drawn to this Gospel. According to Wesley's notations, he preached from the Third Gospel 853 times during his career, fourth in number only to Matthew's Gospel (1,362 recorded usages), Hebrews (965), and the Gospel of John (870).[4] Wesley's heightened interest in money and faith, and more broadly in the character of Christian life, is a key factor here, since this dovetails so well with Luke's own concerns.

Here is an index of sermons Wesley preached from the Third Gospel:

- Sermon 48: "Self-denial" (Luke 9:23)
- Sermon 50: "The Use of Money" (Luke 16:9)
- Sermon 51: "The Good Steward" (Luke 16:2)
- Sermon 67: "Divine Providence" (Luke 12:7)
- Sermon 101: "The Duty of Constant Communion" (Luke 22:19)
- Sermon 115: "Dives and Lazarus" (Luke 16:31)
- Sermon 126: "On Worldly Folly" (Luke 12:20)
- Sermon 146: "The One Thing Needful" (Luke 10:42)
- Sermon 147: "Wiser Than the Children of Light" (Luke 16:8)

What is fascinating about this list is that, of nine sermons posted, four of them come from a single chapter, Luke 16. Why is this significant? It is because Luke 16, from start to finish, emphasizes faithfulness in terms of the right use of wealth.

Wesley as Bible Scholar

Wesley's treatments of Luke 16 and the theme of faith and wealth more broadly deserve special treatment. First, though, Wesley's comments on Luke provide us with an interesting window into one of the more down-to-earth aspects of Wesley as reader of the Bible. Focusing on his sermons and theological treatises, we might overlook how much homework Wesley must have done as a reader of Scripture. He seems to have been the sort of person one might want in a small-group Bible study, a kind of "walking handbook" of background.[5]

We can characterize Wesley the "Bible scholar" in two ways.

On the one hand, we see emerging in his comments the beginnings of an interest in the sort of historical background about which modern biblical studies is most serious.[6] I say "beginnings" because, on the other hand, in his own description of how he engages with biblical texts, we see a decidedly unmodern approach to dealing with difficult texts. "Does anything appear dark or intricate?" he asks. For most of us and our contemporaries, the key to making sense of difficult passages in the Bible is to seek more background, more historical detail, more insight into ancient patterns of behavior. Wesley's approach takes a different path:

> Does anything appear dark or intricate? I lift up my heart to the Father of lights: "Lord, is it not your Word, 'If any lack wisdom, let them ask of God'? You 'give generously and ungrudgingly.' You have said, 'If any be willing to do your will, they shall know.' I am willing to do, let me know, your will." I then search after and consider parallel passages of Scripture, "comparing spiritual things with spiritual." I meditate thereon, with all the attention and earnestness of which my mind is capable. If any doubt still remains, I consult those who are experienced in the things of God, and then the writings whereby, being dead, they yet speak. And what I thus learn, that I teach.[7]

That is, faced with a biblical text that is unclear, Wesley (1) looks to God for help, (2) compares the text with other biblical passages, (3) meditates, (4) consults with "those who are experienced in the things of God," and (5) looks to commentaries and other published works for assistance.[8] This is not to suggest that, for Wesley, historical detail was unimportant. In a stinging reversal of much contemporary biblical interpretation, though, Wesley operates with the assumption that the chief chasm that must be overcome if we are to make sense of Scripture is not measured in terms of our need for more historical detail but with reference to our need to know God and God's ways. "I lift up my heart to the Father of lights. . . . I am willing to do, let me know, your will."

Without wanting to downplay the importance of prayer and theological formation I have just emphasized, let me go on to say that anyone wanting to be schooled in reading the Bible with Wesley must do so by taking advantage of the tools available for doing so. Wesley himself insisted on learning the biblical languages (and the evidence demonstrates that his Greek was quite good, his Hebrew less so), and his biblical studies demonstrate the baseline importance of the critical approaches available to serious readers of the Bible in the 1700s.

True: Wesley aims for "plain truth for plain people." Accordingly, he writes,

> I abstain from all nice and philosophical speculations, from all perplexed and intricate reasonings, and as far as possible from even the show of learning, unless in sometimes citing the original Scriptures. I labor to avoid all words that are not easy to be understood, all which are not used in common life; and in particular those kinds of technical terms that so frequently occur in bodies of divinity, those modes of speaking that persons of reading are intimately acquainted with, but which to common people are an unknown tongue.[9]

But this has to do with how he communicates, not with the sort of homework in which he himself engages. In other words, Wesley's approach to Scripture cannot be characterized as emphasizing prayer over doing research, nor doing research over prayer. He held these together, while obviously prioritizing *the significance of Scripture for Christian faith and life* over the importance of establishing, say, the first-century meaning of a text in its historical context.

What might this mean for Wesleyans? Let me mention three coordinates that follow from this way of reading Scripture: (1) The first question for readers of the Bible concerns *the reader's own interests, allegiances, and character*. Do we come to the Bible ready to hear the voice of God, and to be transformed as we encounter God's voice? (2) Reading the Bible is primarily a *theological task*. Our grasp of the Bible's "truth" is not foremost a question of whether we understand how people back then thought and acted, or whether events reported in the Bible really happened just the way the Bible tells it. These concerns are far too superficial. The question is whether our reading of the Bible coheres with the orthodox faith of the church and inducts us further into the journey of salvation. (3) Whatever tools and approaches to the Bible that do not hinder but encourage these first two coordinates are to be embraced and used. The tools and methods of biblical scholarship are only means to the end of Christian faithfulness—measured in terms of orthodoxy (right belief), orthopraxis (right behavior), and orthokardia (right heart), as we saw in chapter 2.

Discussing these issues is like walking a tightrope. Balance is possible, but hard to maintain. On the one hand, we want to clear the way to appreciate as fully as possible the usefulness of the background knowledge Wesley gives in his study notes. On the other, we want to avoid the trap of imagining that "good" biblical interpretation is primarily about acquiring background knowledge.

Finally, then, let me give a few examples of places where, in his study notes on Luke, Wesley provides background information not readily available in the text itself:

- According to 1:5, Zechariah belongs to the priestly order of Abijah. Wesley explains that priests were divided into twenty-four orders, that Abijah's was the eighth (1 Chr 24:10), and that each order served the temple for seven days with the role of each priest determined by lot.[10] Here and at other points as well, Wesley's notes suggest dependence on the Jewish Mishnah, a codification of oral interpretation of the Law.
- At 1:27 in the Authorized Version, Luke tells us that Mary was "espoused" to Joseph. Translations today sometimes oversimplify by reporting that Mary was "engaged" to Joseph (so the NRSV), but Wesley comments that "it was customary among the Jews for persons that married to contract before witnesses some time before."[11] This helpfully locates Mary in an in-between state called "betrothal"—contractually committed to marry Joseph (so more than what we mean by engagement) but not yet married. This detail is important since it supports the notion that Mary has not yet had sexual relations with Joseph (that is, Mary is a virgin; 1:27, 34), and it prepares for her claim to be a member not of her father's nor of Joseph's household, but of God's (1:38).

- At 10:30, Luke's account of Jesus' parable of the good Samaritan begins, "A certain man went down from Jerusalem to Jericho" (AV). Wesley writes, "The road from Jerusalem to Jericho (about eighteen miles from it) lay through the desert and rocky places: so many robberies and murders were committed therein, that it was called 'the bloody way.' "[12] Wesley's comment gives his readers an insider's perspective on what presumably everyone knew in the first century and heightens the drama of the story.
- At 22:38, one of Jesus' disciples volunteers two swords in response to Jesus' directive that anyone "who has no sword must sell his cloak and buy one" (v. 36). Wesley notes, "Many of Galilee carried them when they traveled, to defend themselves against robbers and assassins, who much infested the roads." Then he adds, "But did the apostles need to seek such defense?" before observing that Jesus "did not mean literally that every one...must have a sword."[13] Why Wesley provided this note is unclear. Was it merely to satisfy a curiosity? Was it to identify these swords as defensive (rather than offensive) weapons? Was he thinking of the traveling conditions in eighteenth-century Britain? In any case, he does not allow this historical conjecture to overshadow the point that, in producing these swords, Jesus' disciples demonstrate their failure to understand Jesus' directive. Jesus' words of reply, "It is enough" (v. 38), are words of exasperation at the dullness of his followers.

Wesley's notes are often of this kind and were a means for providing details that might aid his "plain" or "ordinary" readers. They are sometimes historical and sometimes concerned with the meaning of words or phrases. Sometimes they draw out the meaning of a passage on its own terms and sometimes they treat a passage as though it were written for people in eighteenth-century Britain. To be sure, Wesley observes that many of his notes are not of his own creation and that he drew, sometimes extensively, from others. Chief among these were the historical and grammatical details found in the extensive exegetical annotations of the 1742 publication, *Gnomon of the New Testament,* by the German theologian Johann Albrecht Bengel (1687–1752).[14] By choosing among his sources judiciously, and by translating and publishing them under his own name in his study notes, though, Wesley demonstrates his learning as well as identifies what sort of background he thinks will be helpful to methodist students of the Bible.

Wesley the Preacher on Money

According to the celebrated sermon of Jesus at his home synagogue in Nazareth, Jesus' mission can be summed up in these words: "to preach good news to the poor" (4:18 RSV). The Greek terms for *poor* congregate in the New Testament especially in Luke's Gospel,[15] and Luke includes not only material on wealth and possessions also found in the Gospels of Matthew and Mark but also a number of other passages besides. For example, the parable of the rich man and the story of the poor widow both appear in these three Gospels, but Luke alone has the Song of Mary (1:46-55), the parable of the rich fool (12:13-21), the parable of the shrewd manager (16:1-13), the story of the rich man and Lazarus the beggar (16:19-31), and the story of Zacchaeus (19:1-10). Undoubtedly, then, the Third Gospel tells the story of "good news to the poor," and its definition of discipleship places a special emphasis on the relationship of faith and wealth.

Wesley works with some of this material, and especially with some of the sayings of Jesus in Luke 16. He does not develop how fully this chapter is devoted to questions of Money, so let me summarize:

- Luke 16:1-9: The parable of the shrewd manager opens with the phrase "There was a rich man...," and ends with Jesus' noting the importance of investing the wealth of this world in ways that have eternal consequences.

- Luke 16:10-13: Still speaking to his disciples, Jesus generalizes from the parable of the shrewd manager to emphasize faithful stewardship. He goes on to assert that no one can serve both God and Money. I am capitalizing "money" in order to take seriously that Jesus' concern is not with money per se, but with the power that wealth can wield over us. Either it serves us or we serve it—there is no middle ground.

- Luke 16:11-18: Even though Jesus has been speaking to his disciples (16:1), the Pharisees overhear his words and belittle him. They seem to think that his concern with the poor makes him unfaithful to the law of God. He turns the tables on them, though, in two ways. First, he declares his own faithfulness to the law. Second, he accuses them of breaking the law—not because they have lots of money but because they love money. To put it differently, they love what money brings: prestige, invitations to the right parties, and so on. Jesus is working with a well-known proverb that has it that money is the root of evil (see Acts 20:33; 1 Tim 6:10). Luke *has repeatedly shown* us that the Pharisees are so consumed with their social standing that they exhibit little concern for the plight of the poor (e.g., 11:39-43; 15:1-2). Luke *now tells* his readers the same thing, summarizing in a single expression—"lovers of money"—the greed of the Pharisees, their lack of care for the marginal, and their hyperconcern with status-seeking.

- Luke 16:19-31: Still speaking to the Pharisees, Jesus tells the story of the rich man and Lazarus, which has this punch line: those who are faithful to Moses and the prophets already know and do what God wants in taking care of poor people like this beggar Lazarus.

In short, this whole chapter defines faithful discipleship in a way that brings right into the heart of things our use of money, the value we place on money, and our care for the needy.

Wesley's own approach to these questions is famously represented in his sermon "The Use of Money." Here we find his widely repeated triad: "Gain all you can." "Save all you can." "Give all you can." It will be helpful to put the parable of Luke 16:1-9 before us:

> Then Jesus said to the disciples, "There was a rich man who had a manager, and charges were brought to him that this man was squandering his property. So he summoned him and said to him, 'What is this that I hear about you? Give me an accounting of your management, because you cannot be my manager any longer.' Then the manager said to himself, 'What will I do, now that my master is taking the position away from me? I am not strong enough to dig, and I am ashamed to beg. I have decided what to do so that, when I am dismissed as manager, people may welcome me into their homes.'
>
> "So, summoning his master's debtors one by one, he asked the first, 'How much do you owe my master? He answered, 'A hundred jugs of olive oil.' He said to him, 'Take your bill, sit down quickly, and make it fifty.'
>
> "Then he asked another, 'And how much do you owe?' He replied, 'A hundred containers of wheat.' He said to him, 'Take your bill and make it eighty.'
>
> "And his master commended the dishonest manager because he had acted shrewdly; for the children of this age are more shrewd in dealing with their own generation than are the children of light.
>
> "And I tell you, make friends for yourselves by means of dishonest wealth so that when it is gone, they may welcome you into the eternal homes."

Although the parable of the shrewd manager has puzzled interpreters across time (How could this kind of dishonesty be praised?),[16] Wesley sees immediately the point Jesus is after. People who are guided by the ways of this world know what to do with money. We might say that they read the right newsletters, they study best practices for increasing the financial bottom line, or they excel in pursuing economic gain. They know what to do with money. Why, then, are people who are guided by the ways of the gospel so unwise and unpracticed in what to do with money? To push further, why do people who have declared their allegiance to the ways of Jesus and the kingdom of God continue to follow the ways of this world when it comes to money? Money has become "the grand corrupter of the world, the bane of virtue, the pest of human society" (§2), but this is not the way it has to be. Instead,

> in the hands of his children it is food for the hungry, drink for the thirsty, raiment for the naked. It gives to the traveler and the stranger where to lay their head. By it we may supply the place of a husband to the widow, and of a father to the fatherless; we may be a defense for the oppressed, a means of health to the sick, of ease to them who are in pain. It may be as eyes to the blind, as feet to the lame; indeed, a lifter up from the gates of death. (§2)

How can this be? To this end, Wesley sets for "three plain rules": "Gain all you can." "Save all you can." "Give all you can."

Although Wesley counsels gaining all we can, he immediately rejects ways of making money that are unhealthy, immoral, or harmful to our neighbor. Reflecting very much his own context and concerns, he draws attention to the particular wrongdoing of those in the medical profession who prolong the suffering of others so as to boost their own fees, for example, or who trade in hard liquor (for they traffic in poison and murder, he says). He also rejects forms of employment that contribute to sexual immorality or excessive drinking—"which certainly none can do who has any fear of God, or any real desire of pleasing him."

> It nearly concerns all those to consider this who have anything to do with taverns, victualling-houses, operahouses, play-houses, or any other places of public, fashionable diversion. If these profit the souls of men and women, you are clear; your employment is good, and your gain innocent. But if they are either sinful in themselves, or natural inlets to sin of various kinds, then it is to be feared you have a sad account to make. (§I.6)

But Wesley is as set against laziness and wasting of time as he is against these sorts of jobs. And so by "gaining all you can," he means to say, "Gain all you can by honest industry: use all possible diligence in your calling. Lose no time" (§I.7).

After gaining all they can, Wesley urges followers of Christ to save all they can. Wesley's use of "save," can be misleading, so we might rephrase his counsel with these words: "Rescue all you can." What is Wesley after? He urges his readers to purchase food and clothing for oneself and one's family, together with "whatever nature moderately requires for preserving the body in health and strength" (§III.3). Apart from this, rescue any and all monies from other expenditures, which are surely unnecessary. He explicitly forbids wasting money on what we might call ostentatious spending or uses of money designed to gratify needs beyond what is needed for day-to-day life. His advice on leaving an inheritance for one's children captures well his concerns:

> And why should you throw away money upon your children, any more than upon yourself, in delicate food, in gay or costly apparel, in superfluities of any kind? Why should you purchase for them more pride or lust, more vanity, or foolish and hurtful desires? . . . Why should you be at farther expense to increase their temptations and snares, and to "pierce them through with more sorrows"? . . . Have pity upon them, and remove out of their way what you may easily foresee would increase their sins, and consequently plunge them deeper into everlasting perdition. How amazing then is the infatuation of those parents who think they can never leave their children enough? What! cannot you leave them enough of arrows, firebrands, and death? Not enough of foolish and hurtful desires? Not enough of pride, lust, ambition, vanity? Not enough of everlasting burnings! (§§II.6-7)

Nor, he urges, does "saving all you can" mean putting one's wealth into a bank. *Instead, "saving all you can" means liberating one's money from the fate of sitting idle in a savings account and, especially, rescuing it from habits of spending on what one does not strictly need.*

We can almost hear in the background the words of John the Baptist in Luke's Gospel. Asked what it might mean to demonstrate one's good relationship with God, he announces, "Whoever has two coats must share with anyone who has none; and whoever has food must do likewise" (3:11). Notice how low the bar is set on wealth and sharing with the needy: whoever has two coats, whoever has food (and not, whoever has an overflowing closet, whoever has a full pantry). *"Save all you can,"* Wesley preaches, "by cutting off every expense that serves only to indulge foolish desire, to gratify either the desire of the flesh, the desire of the eye, or the pride of life. Waste nothing, living or dying, on sin or folly, whether for yourself or your children" (§III.6).

Clearly, then, *gaining* and *saving* are not for the purpose of achieving "the good life" or for achieving the status of the upwardly mobile, but so that one might *give*. How much? *"Give all you can,* or in other words give all you have to God" (§III.6). After caring for the immediate needs of one's family, what does one do with the surplus? First, "do good to them that are of the household of faith"; then, if there is more, " 'as you have opportunity, do good to everyone.' In so doing, you give all you can; indeed, in a sound sense, all you have. For all that is laid out in this manner is really given to God" (§III.3).

Basic to Wesley's economic strategy is the image of the steward. When inquiring about how money might be used, he says, we should ask whether we have begun erroneously to imagine that what we have belongs to us, forgetting that all we have actually belongs to God. If so, then we have these mottos: "No more sloth!" "No more waste!" "No more envy!" Then, "give all you have, as well as all you are, a spiritual sacrifice to him who withheld not from you his Son, his only Son; so 'laying up in store for yourselves a good foundation against the time to come, that you may have eternal life'" (§III.7).

Questions for Reflection and Discussion

1. The Gospel of Luke is very much concerned about Jesus as Savior. Being saved presumes that we need to be saved from something. What do you need to be saved from? Pride? Envy? Laziness? Anger? Lying? Gossiping? Dishonesty? Overindulging?
2. In Luke we see how Jesus healed and taught. But his healing and teaching were not meant to be ends in and of themselves, but to serve a greater purpose—God's purpose. What do you think God's purpose was for the people Jesus healed and taught? How might that purpose be valid for people today?

3. Through Jesus, God widened God's love to include all people, even the last, least, and lost, whether or not they were Jews. How is your ministry as a believer and as part of the church widening the circle of God's love? Who else do you need to include?

4. If you understand that Jesus offers you his friendship, what might that mean for you? If Jesus is your friend, how can you count on him? How can he count on you?

5. Many people find it difficult to talk about money, especially in church. Why do you think this is? Is it true in your own experience?

6. If we align our spending habits with God's purpose, how would your budget look? your church's budget? Do you believe that tithing is a worthy spiritual discipline?

7. John Wesley was very specific about his views concerning money. He saw money as a possible obstacle to one's faith development. How can money help and hurt us? Does how we spend our money say something about what we value? Looking at your spending, what does it say about what you value?

8. From a Wesleyan perspective, Bible study should draw us into a deeper relationship with God. What steps can you take to be more disciplined in your study? From Wesley's point of view, what is a biblical expert? Are you willing to be open to hearing God as you study the Scriptures?

4

Gospel of John

Turning the pages of their New Testaments to the Fourth Gospel, the Gospel of John, readers of the Gospels of Matthew, Mark, and Luke will find themselves on terrain both familiar and strange. The Fourth Gospel has as its main character the same Jesus we encounter in the other three, and the ministry of this Jesus is set against the same backdrop of the life of the Jewish people under Roman rule. But there are differences, too. The first three Gospels are often called "Synoptic" Gospels because they sketch the ministry and message of Jesus according to a "common view" (Greek: *synoptikos*). According to this way of thinking, John's "view" of Jesus is "uncommon," set apart from the others. Recalling that more than 95 percent of the material found in Mark's Gospel is also found in the Gospels of Matthew and Luke, it is worth noting that the overlap in material between Mark's Gospel and John's extends to only about 5 percent.

For example, in the Synoptic Gospels, Jesus teaches in parables. With a few remarkable exceptions, his teaching segments are relatively short, often given in summary fashion, and ranging across a wide array of topics, such as prayer, wealth and possessions, marriage and divorce, and faith. In the Synoptic Gospels, Jesus is known as an exorcist and miracle worker. In the Gospel of John, though, we find no parables, Jesus addresses his disciples and others in lengthy, well-developed sermons, he performs no exorcisms, and his miracles are regarded as "signs." In the Synoptic Gospels, Jesus proclaims the kingdom of God; in John's Gospel, kingdom-language is rare and Jesus speaks of himself instead. None of the famous "I am" statements made by Jesus in the

Gospel of John appear in the Synoptics. In the Synoptic Gospels, Jesus' miracles reveal the inbreaking kingdom of God; in John's Gospel, Jesus' signs reveal Jesus' glory. In the Synoptic Gospels, Jesus' identity is generally kept secret and he is slow to use titles other than "Son of Man" when speaking of himself; in John's Gospel, Jesus speaks openly of himself in terms of his unique identity as Son of God. John's Gospel has Jesus making the trek to Jerusalem three times, and from this we tend to think that Jesus' public mission lasted three years. He is in Jerusalem as an adult only once in the other Gospels,[1] and the Gospel of Mark in particular moves through Jesus' public mission so quickly that, read in isolation from John's Gospel, we might have imagined that Jesus' ministry spanned only a few months.

The differences between John's Gospel and the Synoptics may surprise first-time readers of the New Testament, but they have long been recognized by the church. For example, the early church theologian Clement of Alexandria (*ca.* A.D. 150–215) perceived the differences and thought them worthy of explanation. So he wrote that, among the four New Testament Gospels, John wrote last. According to Clement, John recognized that the public significance of Jesus had been made plain in the Gospels of Matthew, Luke, and Mark, so he composed a Gospel that made plain the significance of Jesus from God's perspective.[2] So remarkable is the uniqueness of John's narrative when compared to the Synoptics that Clement went on to add that the Evangelist was both encouraged by his friends and inspired by the Spirit to write his Gospel.

The unease that these differences caused among some in the early church is also reflected in Origen's (*ca.* A.D. 185–254) *Commentary on John*. There, he details some of the ways in which John differs from the Synoptics before insisting that the key to making sense of these differences had to do with how we interpret these books. Faced with these differences, we should not try to harmonize the Gospel accounts, any more than we should choose to follow one Gospel while neglecting the other three. Instead, we should take seriously their different perspectives and read them in ways that honor them. We should accept all four Gospels, recognizing that their truth does not lie in what Origen calls "the outward and material letter"[3] —that is, in terms of the details about what Jesus did and when he did it. In the midst of differences at the literal level, or at the level of the narratives themselves, their truth lies instead in their ability to give us access to God's perspective on the significance of Jesus' life and ministry. This is their inner, spiritual meaning.

It may be hard for us today to get our heads around this way of thinking about the "spiritual" meaning of these texts. Imagine, though, a time when everything—the words on the page, the rocks on a path, the animals in the wild, the stars in the sky—was understood not only as God's work but as a visible symbol of God's character and will. In such a time, whether "water" could be represented as H_2O was not nearly so important as what water might tell us about God. In fact, in the ancient world, "living water" referred to flowing or springwater as opposed to still water from a well or cistern, but this does not keep John's Gospel from using the phrase to refer to salvation from God (as in the story of the Samaritan woman—see 4:10-15). Or to take an example from Origen, John's Gospel has the cleansing of the Temple early on in the public career of Jesus (2:14-22), but the Synoptics have it during the last week of Jesus' life (e.g., Mark 11:15-17). This gives the early church theologian opportunity to reflect on the spiritual significance of the event in John, and he does not disappoint. For example, Jesus drives out the animals because he anticipates the time, following his death, when temple sacrifices will be unnecessary. Moreover, expelling the animals from the temple represents the expulsion of the lower, earthy, base parts of the human being from the more high-minded and lofty. Origen goes on to claim that Jesus should have been attacked or arrested for his behavior in the Temple; that he was not is proof of his divine nature.[4] And all of this is true even if the event John recounts did not actually take place at the time when John records it.

Such interpretations were generally not available by the time of Wesley, since Protestant churches generally and some parts of the Roman Catholic Church had moved away from this way of thinking in favor of a primary or sole interest in the "literal" meaning of Scripture. In fact, Wesley seems not to notice that John's location of the Temple cleansing earlier rather than later in the narrative of Jesus' life might raise questions. Instead, his notes clarify what John might have taken for granted: the animals were used for sacrifice, the money-changers performed a needed service by exchanging foreign currency into local currency, and, according to Wesley's reading of John's story, Jesus actually struck no one, not even the animals.[5]

Given the premium placed on "literal" interpretation (and the general rejection of "spiritual" interpretation) among Protestants, we might have anticipated that John Wesley would have avoided the route taken by either Clement or Origen. And this is the case. If Clement, Origen, and others saw the differences between John and the Synoptic Gospels as a challenge to the church and its reading of the Gospels, this does not seem to have been the case for Wesley. Wesley does, however, emphasize the *theological* character of the Fourth Gospel. Thus, he prefaces his notes on the Gospel of John with this description: "In this book is set down the history of the Son of God dwelling among humankind."[6] Note Wesley's reference to "the Son of God" rather than, say, "the man Jesus of Nazareth." Moreover, he refers to John's Gospel as a "supplement" to the Synoptics,[7] thus acknowledging that John could go his own way because he was able to assume what was written already in the other three narratives of Jesus' life and mission.

If we find in Wesley's study notes much more in the way of explicit theological work than would be true of Wesley's comments on the Synoptic Gospels, this reflects the interests of the Gospel of John itself. Wesley's understanding of the human need for and experience of salvation comes very much to the fore in his sermons on John as well as in his notes, as does his understanding of the significance of Jesus (that is, his Christology). Although Wesley preached hundreds of times from the Gospel of John, he seems not to have prepared hundreds of different sermons or to have drawn from the many texts to which a preacher might turn in the Fourth Gospel. His sermons include these:

- Sermon 18: "The Marks of the New Birth" (John 3:8)
- Sermon 45: "The New Birth" (John 3:7)
- Sermon 46: "The Wilderness State" (John 16:22)

- Sermon 90: "An Israelite Indeed" (John 1:47)
- Sermon 138A: "On Dissimulation" (John 1:47)
- Sermon 140: "The Promise of Understanding" (John 13:7)

Among these, clearly the most popular had to do with the new birth (Sermons 18, 45) and what we might call the experience of spiritual dryness—that is, the loss of faith, love, joy, and peace that sometimes happens when those who have experienced new birth find that doubt has taken up residence in their lives (Sermon 46).

Wesley and the New Birth

Given the nature of the renewal movement Wesley helped to spearhead, he was repeatedly drawn in his thinking and preaching to Jesus' words to Nicodemus in John 3:3: "Very truly, I tell you, no one can see the kingdom of God without being born from above"—rendered in Wesley's Authorized Version in these terms: "Verily, verily, I say unto thee, Except a man be born again, he cannot see the kingdom of God." The most noticeable difference between these two translations is their reading of the Greek adverb *anōthen*, which can refer to an event that originates "from above" as well as to an event that happens "anew." In fact, the best translation would somehow incorporate both ideas, since the "birth" about which Jesus speaks is clearly a second birth, though not one that merely repeats the first. Readers of the Fourth Gospel have known since its opening paragraphs that what is needed is to be born from above—that is, to become children of God. Thus, writes the Evangelist, "To all who received him, who believed in his name, he gave power to become children of God, who were born, not of blood or of the will of the flesh or of the will of man, but of God" (1:12-13). In the dialogue between Jesus and Nicodemus, Jesus places the emphasis on the spatial metaphor ("born from above"), whereas Nicodemus emphasizes the temporal side of things ("born a second time"). For this reason, Nicodemus struggles to understand how an adult "can . . . enter a second time into the mother's womb and be born" (3:4).

The metaphor of rebirth is not unique to the Gospel of John, but is found elsewhere in the biblical tradition and beyond. Paul's image of "new creation" (2 Cor 5:17; Gal 6:15; see already Isa 65:17) is closely related, as is the metaphor of being adopted into a new family (e.g., Rom 8:14-17). The letter of James refers to the power of the gospel ("the true word," Jas 1:18; my translation) in the birthing of followers of Christ. In the letter to Titus, baptism is interpreted in terms of "the water of rebirth and renewal by the Holy Spirit" (3:5). And 1 Peter takes up the language of "new birth" explicitly:

> Blessed be the God and Father of our Lord Jesus Christ, who in accordance with his great mercy has given us new birth into a living hope through the resurrection of Jesus Christ from the dead, into an imperishable, uncorrupted, and unfading inheritance, reserved in heaven for you who are guarded by God's power through his faithfulness for a salvation ready to be revealed at the last time.[8] (1:3-4; see 2:2-3)

Although each of these NT writings develops this imagery in its own ways, there are some common motifs that hold them together. These would include:

- Salvation is a gift from God. We do not push the metaphor too far when we recognize that no one gives birth to oneself.
- Salvation is personalized in terms of human transformation. Life is begun anew, with growth in grace anticipated of the newly born.
- Salvation incorporates the believer into a community of others who have been born anew—that is, into the family of God. In other words, believers now take their identity both from God and from their relationships within the community of God's people. Here there is no room for the social distinctions that divide humans according to status, for all are siblings serving the same God within the same family.
- Salvation locates the reborn within the grand mural of God's saving purpose in the world, whether this is un-

derstood in terms of "seeing the kingdom" (as in John 3), for example, or in terms of "new creation" (as in Paul). We grasp the world differently because we relate to it differently. As Paul put it, "Everything old has passed away; see, everything has become new!" (2 Cor 5:17).

- Salvation involves being nurtured in new ways of thinking, feeling, believing, and behaving appropriate to one's new allegiance to God. The newly born experience the world according to fresh patterns and respond accordingly. What does Jesus mean when he says that "no one can see the kingdom of God without being born from above" (John 3:3)? Only those who can see and really see, who see what can be seen only with the insight of faith, are able to discern what God is doing in the world.

- Salvation entails being a child of God in a secondary sense. We can be God's children because of the work of God's Son, Jesus Christ.

Wesley's notes on John 3 indicate the central role he allotted the exchange between Jesus and Nicodemus in Wesley's presentation of the human situation and the order of salvation. On John 3:3 he writes:

> In this solemn discourse our Lord shows that no external profession, no ceremonial ordinances, or privileges of birth, could entitle any to the blessings of the Messiah's kingdom: that an entire change of heart, as well as of life, was necessary for that purpose; that this could only be wrought in a person by the almighty power of God; that every person born into the world was by nature in a state of sin, condemnation, and misery; that the free mercy of God had given his Son to deliver them from it, and to raise them to a blessed immortality; that all humankind, Gentiles as well as Jews, might share in these benefits, procured by his being lifted up on the cross, and to be received by faith in him; but that, if they rejected him, their eternal, aggravated condemnation would be the certain consequence.[9]

Following this, on John 3:7, he writes, "To be born again is to be inwardly changed from all sinfulness to all holiness."[10]

Before unpacking Wesley's notion of the "new birth" further, it is worth hesitating for a moment in order to draw attention to what he is doing here as an interpreter of the Bible. I have already observed that Wesley was a child of the Protestant Reformation in embracing the plain sense of the biblical text. "You are in danger of enthusiasm every hour," he wrote, "if you depart ever so little from Scripture; yea, or from the plain, literal meaning of any text, taken in connection with the context."[11] Note that, in Wesley's day, as in this quotation from one of Wesley's pamphlets, "enthusiasm" could refer to unrestrained religious extremism. In this case, then, Wesley urges that the preventative of (or antidote to) the dangers of "enthusiasm" was taking the text on its own terms within its own context. But the careful reader of Wesley's comments on John 3:3 will notice right away that Wesley has not simply followed his own advice. We know this because he has sketched the human situation and the promises of salvation in terms that far exceed what we read either in this verse, or even in this third chapter of John, or even in the whole of the Gospel of John. Clearly, something else is going on here.

That something else can be understood in a couple of ways. One is to imagine that Wesley has extended what he means by a "plain sense" reading of the text to include the plain sense of a text *when read within the framework of the church's theology*. Another is to imagine that Wesley has extended what he means by "context" *to include the ecclesial (or "churchly") context within which Christians read Scripture*. Either way, we can see that Wesley thinks that the meaning of this text is clear enough when set within the frame of his well-developed theology of salvation (that is, his "soteriology," a word formed from joining the two Greek words *soterion* ["salvation"] and *logos* ["understanding"]).

Let me put this differently. Wesley's interest in a "literal sense" departs in a crucial way from the modern quest for the single, intended meaning of a biblical text. Since the eighteenth century, study of the Bible has tended to think of the meaning of a text in terms of its historical sense, and especially with reference to what the original human authors intended as they wrote. This way of thinking has even become codified in our dictionaries, where we find definitions that link "meaning" to a speaker's "intentions."

For Wesley, though, the human authors of biblical texts did not possess that sort of veto power when grappling with the meaning of texts they had penned. Instead, the reader of the Bible must contend with the ultimate Author of Scripture. This is God alone. Recently, Brevard Childs has made a similar point, writing that "the literal sense was never restricted to a verbal, philological exercise alone, but functioned for both Jews and Christians as a 'ruled reading' in which a balance was struck between a grammatical reading and the structure of communal practice or a 'rule of faith' (*regula fidei*)."[12] For Wesley, the "literal sense" coincided with the general tenor of Scripture. He thus emphasized, on the one hand, reading a biblical text within the whole of Scripture, and, on the other, reading a biblical text against the backdrop of what Childs refers to as the "rule of faith," but what Wesley called "the analogy of faith." This refers to those doctrinal affirmations that arise from the biblical texts themselves, which are then used to guide faithful readings of the Bible. For Wesley, the analogy of faith concerns above all the Christian affirmation of the triune God and the order of salvation with its emphasis on sin, free grace, and holiness of heart and life.

How this works out in Wesley's work on John 3 is seen easily enough from his two sermons "The New Birth" (John 3:7) and "The Marks of the New Birth" (John 3:8). Wesley begins the first by distinguishing between two fundamental Christian "doctrines": "the doctrine of justification, and that of the new birth: the former relating to that great work which God does *for us*, in forgiving our sins; the latter to the great work which God does *in us*, in renewing our fallen nature" (§1). From this beginning, he moves on to address three questions: (1) Why must we be born again? (2) How must we be born again? (3) To what end are we born again?

(1) Why must we be born again? Wesley grounds our need for new birth in the accounts of humanity's creation and fall in Genesis 1 and 3. Humanity was made in the divine image:

"God is love": accordingly humanity at creation was full of love, which was the sole principle of all the human's tempers, thoughts, words, and actions. God is full of justice, mercy, and truth: so was humankind as humanity came from the hands of the Creator. God is spotless purity: and so humanity was in the beginning pure from every sinful blot. Otherwise God could not have pronounced humankind as well as all the other works of his hands, "very good." (§I.1)

However, humans were created with the ability to stand but the possibility of falling. God warned humanity of this possibility, but humanity ate of the forbidden tree. And as God had warned, "accordingly in that day humanity did die: humankind died to God, the most dreadful of all deaths." Accordingly, the human family "lost both the knowledge and the love of God," "became unholy as well as unhappy," and sank "into pride and self-will" (§I.2). Rebelling against God had as its consequence nothing less than "the loss of the life and image of God" (§I.3).

(2) How must we be born again? Wesley develops his understanding of the new birth by analogy with the birth of a newborn baby. Working with the medical understanding of his day, he claims that, prior to birth, a baby has ears but cannot hear, eyes but cannot see, and so on. But at the point of birth, babies enter into a world altogether different from the one they had previously occupied, and therefore live an entirely different kind of life. Speaking spiritually, the same can be said. Before being born anew, people have spiritual eyes and ears, but "a thick impenetrable veil lies upon them" (§II.4). "We have no reliable knowledge of the things of God, of the Spirit and eternity. Though one is a living person, one is not yet alive as a Christian."[13] With the new birth, then, we experience a total change. Our ears and eyes are opened, our senses are attuned to God, we feel the peace of God in our hearts, we grow in the grace and knowledge of God. Indeed, "such a person may be properly said to be alive"—awakened by God's Spirit, now alive to God through Jesus Christ.[14] The new birth is that change "when the love of the world is changed into the love of God, pride into humility, passion into meekness, hatred and malice into a sincere, tender, disinterested love for all humankind" (§II.5).

(3) To what end are we born again? Another way to put this question is, Why is new birth necessary? Wesley's answer is simple: the new birth is necessary if we are to be holy.

For what is holiness, according to the oracles of God? Not a bare external religion, a round of outward duties, however many they be, and however exactly performed. No; gospel holiness is no less than the image of God stamped upon the heart. It is no other than the whole mind which was in Christ Jesus. It consists of all heavenly affections and tempers mingled together in one. It implies such a continual, thankful love to him who hath not withheld from us his Son, his only Son, as makes it natural, and in a manner necessary to us, to love everyone.... It is such a love of God as teaches us to be blameless in all manner of conversation; as enables us to present ourselves, all we are and all we have, all our thoughts, words, and actions, a continual sacrifice to God, acceptable through Christ Jesus. (§III.1)

For Wesley, this and more is meant by holiness, and this description of the holy person can be true of no one who is not born anew.

But there is more. The new birth is necessary for eternal life, for only those who share in God's holiness (made possible through new birth) share in God's glory. Apart from new birth, true happiness in this world is not possible. This is because holiness is necessary for happiness. Wesley writes that "malice, hatred, envy, jealousy, revenge, create a present hell in the breast," just as "sin, pride, self-will, and idolatry, are, in the same proportion as they prevail, general sources of misery. Therefore as long as these reign in any soul happiness has no place there. But they must reign till the bent of our nature is changed, that is, until we are born again. Consequently the new birth is absolutely necessary in order to have happiness in this world, as well as in the world to come" (§III.3).

Wesley's sermon continues as he draws out some of the inferences of his message on the new birth. Chief among these are two—that the new birth is not the same as baptism, though it is assumed that those who have been born anew will also be "born of water" (John 3:5); and that the new birth cannot be identified with sanctification. New birth "is a part of sanctification, not the whole; it is the gate of it, the entrance into it. When we are born again, then our sanctification, our inward and outward holiness, begins. And thenceforward we are gradually to "grow up in him who is our head." Here Wesley returns to the analogy with the birth of a child:

> A child is born of a woman in a moment, or at least in a very short time. Afterward the child gradually and slowly grows into adulthood. In like manner a child is born of God in a short time, if not in a moment. But it is by slow degrees that the child of God afterward grows up to the measure of the full stature of Christ. The same relation therefore which there is between our natural birth and our growth there is also between our new birth and our sanctification. (§IV.3)

At this point, we begin to touch on the burden of Wesley's second sermon from John 3, in which he seeks to set out plainly the marks of those who have in fact been born anew. Here we find an engaging treatise on what have long been known as the three theological virtues: faith, hope, and love. Constructing a virtual collage of scriptural texts, Wesley summarizes:

> It is so to believe in God through Christ as "not to commit sin" [1 John 3:9], and to enjoy, at all times and in all places, that "peace of God that passes all understanding" [Phil 4:7]. It is so to hope in God through the Son of his love as to have not only the "testimony of a good conscience" [2 Cor 1:12], but also "the Spirit of God bearing witness with your spirits that you are the children of God" [Rom 8:16]: whence cannot but spring the "rejoicing evermore in him through whom you have received the atonement" [1 Thess 5:16]. It is so to love God, who has thus loved you, as you never did love any creature: so that ye are constrained to love everyone as yourselves; with a love not only ever burning in your hearts, but flaming out in all your actions and conversations, and making your whole life one "labor of love" [1 Thess 1:3], one continued obedience to those commands, "Be merciful, as God is merciful" [Luke 6:36]; "Be holy, as I the Lord am holy" [1 Pet 1:16]: "Be perfect, as your Father which is in heaven is perfect" [Matt 5:48].

Given my earlier comments about Wesley's notion of a "plain sense" reading of the Bible, it should not surprise us to see how, in this last paragraph, Wesley has expanded on what it means to be "born of the Spirit" (John 3:8) without a single reference to any other text within the Gospel of John. After all, he himself noted at the beginning of the sermon that his purpose in expounding the new birth was "to lay down the marks of it in the plainest manner, just as I find them laid down in Scripture" (§2). Here, clearly, we are at the heart of the message of Scripture, according to Wesley. We can almost hear him declare that faith, hope, and love serve to define "the general tenor of Scripture," for they are found on every page of the Bible.

The prayer with which Wesley closes his sermon "On the Marks of the New Birth" invites meditation:

> Amen, Lord Jesus! May all who prepare their hearts yet again to seek your face receive again that Spirit of adoption, and cry out, Abba, Father! Let them now again have power to believe in your name as to become children of God; as to know and feel they have "redemption in your blood, even the forgiveness of sins," and that they "cannot commit sin, because they are born of God." Let them be now "born again unto a living hope," so as to "purify themselves, as you are pure"! And "because they are children," let the Spirit of love and of glory rest upon them, cleansing them "from all filthiness of flesh and spirit," and teaching them to "perfect holiness in the fear of God"!

Questions for Reflection and Discussion

1. The Gospel of John is significantly different from Matthew, Mark, and Luke. What difference does it make? How does this difference add to our understanding of Jesus and of our salvation?
2. Reflect on your own experience of being a new creation in Christ. What does it mean to be born again?
3. Salvation is a gift from God for each of us, personally, that incorporates a believer into the family of God—the church. It gives us new allegiances, values, purposes, and goals as evidenced in our behaviors both as individuals and as a community of faith; and it is only the result of the life, death, and resurrection of Jesus. What does your salvation mean to you in your everyday living?
4. According to Wesley, holiness leads to happiness and in sharing the glory of God. For Wesley the holy person is not a dour, grim, or sad person, deprived of warmth. The holy person is the

personification of God's grace. Who in your experience would you consider to be a holy person? Does this vision of holiness differ from yours?

5. God created humanity with the ability to stand, albeit with the possibility of falling. But God is always there to help us back to our feet. Looking at your own life, where have you stood tall and where have you fallen? What and who helped you get back on your feet? How have you helped others get back on their feet?

6. If salvation is the most important thing God offers us, what does that say about how we are to value offering God's salvation to others? Suggestion: make a list of persons who have no apparent relationship with Christ and pray for each daily for a year.

7. If a relationship with God through Jesus Christ is an imperative, how can your church reach out to others? How welcoming is your church, your small group, your family? How might Jesus be calling you to widen God's circle of love today?

5

Acts of the Apostles

In the New Testament, the book of Acts is unique in providing a narrative bridge from the story of Jesus to the story of the early church. The four Gospels end with stories of the empty tomb of Jesus. The Gospels of Matthew, Luke, and John each record appearances of Jesus to his followers and in various ways commission those followers to carry on the mission of Jesus. Jesus' final words in Matthew are often repeated as the "Great Commission":

> And Jesus came and said to them, "All authority in heaven and on earth has been given to me. Go therefore and make disciples of all nations, baptizing them in the name of the Father and of the Son and of the Holy Spirit, and teaching them to obey everything that I have commanded you. And remember, I am with you always, to the end of the age." (Matt 28:18-20)

The words of Jesus in Luke's Gospel are similar. There, Jesus grounds the necessity of the disciples' mission in Israel's Scriptures and declares that they will be empowered for mission by the Holy Spirit promised by God. Accordingly, "Repentance and forgiveness of sins is to be proclaimed in [the name of Christ] to all nations, beginning from Jerusalem" (Luke 24:47). Early in the Acts of the Apostles, these notes are sounded again. Speaking to his followers, Jesus claims that "you will receive power when the Holy Spirit has come upon you; and you will be my witnesses in Jerusalem, in all Judea and Samaria, and to the ends of the earth" (Acts 1:8). In this way, the author of Acts, whom tradition identifies as Luke, indicates how profoundly the story of Jesus leads into the story of the early church. The basis of this continuity lies in the work of Jesus, and then in the empowerment of the Holy Spirit and the missional definition of the church. What holds the story together, finally, is the one purpose of God to bring salvation in all its fullness to all people.

Wesley understood that the Gospel of Luke and the Acts of the Apostles were written by the same author, but spoke of the role of the book of Acts less as a continuation of the Third Gospel and more as the continuation of the story of the Gospels read as a whole.

> This book, in which St. Luke records the actions of the apostles, particularly of St. Peter and St. Paul, . . . is as it were the center between the Gospels and the Epistles. It contains after a very brief recapitulation of the evangelical history, a continuation of the history of Christ, the event of his predictions, and a kind of supplement to what he before spoke to his disciples by the Holy Spirit now given to them.

Then, using a botanical image, he writes that Acts "contains also the seeds and first stamina [that is, the pollen-producing part of a flower] of all those things that are enlarged upon in the Epistles."[1]

The case for the particular relationship between the Third Gospel and the Acts of the Apostles is easy to make on the basis of the prefaces to these two books:

Luke 1:1-4	Acts 1:1-2
Since many have undertaken to set down an orderly account of the events that have been fulfilled among us, just as they were handed on to us by those who from the beginning were eyewitnesses and servants of the word, I too decided, after investigating everything carefully from the very first, to write an orderly account for you, most excellent Theophilus, so that you may know the truth concerning the things about which you have been instructed.	In the first book, Theophilus, I wrote about all that Jesus did and taught from the beginning until the day when he was taken up to heaven, after giving instructions through the Holy Spirit to the apostles whom he had chosen.

From the first words of Acts, then, we see that this narrative is a continuation of a former book. The rest of the preface ensures that we understand that this "former book" was the Gospel of Luke (and not, say, the Gospel of John). At the beginning of both books, Luke mentions Theophilus, who was probably a real person whose status in the Roman world would assist Luke in getting his narrative "published." I mention that Theophilus was a real person because his name means "lover of God," and it is possible that Luke identifies in this way his audience as "God lovers." However, the name Theophilus was very much in use in the first century, and we have no evidence to suggest that these sorts of "literary dedications" were made to anything but real people.

If Acts follows on from Luke, we might wonder why they have come to us as two separate books. The bottom line is that it was simply impossible to present both Luke and Acts in a single "volume." Luke's Gospel has about 19,400 words and Acts has about 18,400, so each would have required its own papyrus roll of some thirty-five feet. But, when gluing together sheets of papyrus side by side, the maximum length for a scroll would have been about thirty-five feet. Separating Luke and Acts, then, was a technological necessity. It is therefore interesting that Luke and Acts are symmetrical not only in length but also in the span of years covered (about thirty years), and in the fact that, just as the account of Jesus' suffering and death comprises some 25 percent of the Gospel, so Paul's arrest and trials account for some 25 percent of Acts. Theologically, the ascension of Jesus, narrated both at the end of the Gospel and the beginning of Acts, serves as the hinge on which Luke's narrative turns. Together with Jesus' resurrection, the ascension is also the theological focal point of the narrative, which repeatedly emphasizes the importance of Jesus' exaltation for our salvation. Taken together, the writings of Luke comprise the single largest contribution to the New Testament (28 percent of the whole).

Already in the second century, Luke's Gospel came to circulate with the Gospels of Matthew, Mark, and John, together forming the fourfold Gospel canon. Acts, on the other hand, found its home in relation to the New Testament letters, especially those written by Paul. Now securely located between the Gospels and the collections of letters in the New Testament, the book of Acts plays two important roles. The first, which Wesley also recognized, is that Acts ensures that there is no gap in the story line from the life, death, and resurrection of Jesus to the birth, mission, and growth of the church. Acts shows how the movement initiated by Jesus in Galilee and Judea developed into communities of believers and missionary activity spread across the Roman Empire. What is more, if we read the New Testament from start to finish, from left to right, then Acts provides a perspective from which to make sense of the letters the New Testament.

The hero of Acts is clearly Paul, who carries the gospel to the Gentiles and suffers because of it. Acts undergirds the spread of the good news to the Gentiles throughout the world, and it authorizes the work of particular witnesses, including Peter and James, but especially Paul. In addition, the book of Acts fills in the background for understanding a number of people, places, and events mentioned explicitly and presupposed in the New Testament letters. Without Luke's historical narrative, it would be hard to follow the timetable and movement of Paul's missionary activity, for example, and we would know next to nothing about the roles of Peter the apostle and James the brother of Jesus in the earliest days of the Christian movement.

The Missionary Character of Acts

We have from Wesley three sermons that take as their starting point the book of Acts:

- Sermon 2: "The Almost Christian" (Acts 26:28)
- Sermon 4: "Scriptural Christianity" (Acts 4:31)
- Sermon 37: "The Nature of Enthusiasm" (Acts 26:24)

As with Wesley's sermons more generally, this count is deceptive since he has peppered numerous sermons with phrases and illustrations from the Acts of the Apostles. This is especially true of his interest in the nature of the Christian community which Luke describes in two summary passages, Acts 2:42-47 and 4:32-35. We will return to this emphasis momentarily.

Given the nature of the Wesleyan movement, Acts may be most

significant for its missional emphasis. This is underscored in part by Sermon 4, "Scriptural Christianity." Without following the outline of Acts itself, Wesley nonetheless traces the spread of "scriptural Christianity" in ever-increasing circles, from its beginnings with individual human beings to its spread from one person to the next, and finally to its covering the whole earth. Acts 1:8 testifies to a similar interest in the spread of the good news, though it uses geographical terms rather than personal ones: "You will receive power when the Holy Spirit has come upon you; and you will be my witnesses in Jerusalem, in all Judea and Samaria, and to the ends of the earth."

Since geography is socially defined space, we ought not to think that Luke is marking the spread of the good news in terms of mere points or boundaries on an ancient map. Jerusalem, for example, is the place of the Temple, God's house, so its importance on an ancient map would be pivotal—that is, for those who acknowledged the God of Israel, Jerusalem would have been pivotal. If Jerusalem is thus the center of the earth, then the movement to Judea, Samaria, and the end of the earth is about moving farther and farther away from the center. This is especially clear when we understand the meaning of "the end of the earth" (the Greek term for "end" in 1:8, *eschatos,* is singular, but the NRSV has translated it as though it were plural, "ends"). For the ancient Roman geography, Strabo, "the end of the earth" might refer to Ethiopia, for example, or northern Europe or Spain. In Luke's "Bible," though, and especially for Isaiah, "the end of the earth" is less easy to pinpoint on a map: it is "everywhere," "among all peoples," "across all boundaries." Especially important is Isaiah 49:6, in which the Lord says to his servant: "It is too light a thing that you should be my servant to raise up the tribes of Jacob and to restore the survivors of Israel; I will give you as a light to the nations, that my salvation may reach to the end of the earth." In this passage, "the nations" parallels "the end of the earth," so that when Isaiah 49:6 is quoted in Acts 13:47, "the end of the earth" refers to "the Gentiles."[2] Indeed, Luke reports that Paul and Barnabas quoted the Isaianic text in order to support their decision, "We are now turning to the Gentiles" (Acts 13:46). In other words, the Spirit-empowered mission crosses all social and religious boundaries to include everyone, Jew and Gentile.

Understood in this way, Acts 1:8 is not so much an outline of the book of Acts as it is a missionary mandate. Those who follow Jesus' commission are witnesses to Jesus in ever-increasing circles, crossing lines of all kinds in order to embrace people with the good news. This is why Paul is so clearly the hero of Acts: he does what Jesus said to do. Note the terms of the commission Paul receives from the Lord: "He is an instrument whom I have chosen to bring my name before Gentiles and kings and before the people of Israel" (Acts 9:15). And this is exactly what Paul begins to do when he joins Barnabas at Antioch and both are sent out into the predominately Gentile world (see Acts 13–14).

The outline of Acts is actually determined by the repetition of a key phrase in the story: "the word of God grew." This phrase appears in Acts 6:7; 12:24; 19:20, each time marking the end of conflict, signaling the advance of the missionary movement in the midst of persecution, and anticipating the next major development in the narrative. Luke thus marks the progression of "the word" in four stages: the mission in Jerusalem (Acts 1:15–6:7), expansion from Jerusalem to Antioch (6:8–12:25), expansion from Antioch to Asia and Europe (13:1–19:20), and finally the journeys of Paul the missionary prisoner (19:21–28:31). Why this emphasis on the "growth" of the word? This way of putting things is rooted in Jesus' parable of the sower in Luke 8:4-15, which emphasizes the effects of the word. The word is like the seed that Jesus and his followers broadcast, which leads to the production and growth of the people of God. But if the story line of the book of Acts is built around the sowing and growth of God's word, this is just another way of saying that the book of Acts is concerned from start to finish with the mission of the church and, then, with how the missionary church puts on display the word as it matures among its people—all as empowered by the Holy Spirit poured out at Pentecost.

For good reason, then, in his sermon "Scriptural Christianity" Wesley can ask where those people are who are filled with the Spirit. Indeed, he directly asks his audience if they themselves are a community filled with the Spirit. As he explains, this would be evidenced in their love of God and neighbor and in such practices as their care of the needy and spreading the good news to others.

Wesley and the "History" of Acts

Wesley's "explanatory notes" on the Acts of the Apostles gives us a pretty clear window into what he thought about the narrative Luke has provided. Most of his comments fill in the background with historical details or provide brief notes to ensure that his readers are able to make sense of the story as it develops. He appears to take Acts as a straightforward history of what happened, with the result that he has little to say about how Acts presents the overarching work of God. This is not surprising, since this is largely the approach readers took to Acts until fairly recently.

We can fill out how best to think about Acts by asking the question, What does it mean to say that Acts is a "history" of the early church? Since the nineteenth century, many of us in the West have been taught to expect from historians a kind of investigative work concerned with "just the facts." However, the truth is that none of us could ever report "what actually happened," since such a report would require an all-knowing perspective and would be impossibly full of unnecessary and unwanted details. In reality, historians are not interested simply in "what really happened," but in what they and their communities deem to be significant among the many things that might have been recorded. They are also concerned with how these events are related to each other.

One way to grasp what Luke has done is to recognize that the history of the early church might have been told differently—by different historians with different emphases. For example, others might have told the story by focusing less on Jerusalem and Rome, more on Antioch or Philippi. Why does Peter disappear in the second half of Acts? What is he doing while Paul's mission moves west, or while Paul is on trial? What stories might have been told about James, Jesus' brother? Or consider this: we can be sure that the Jewish leadership in Jerusalem interpreted what was going on in ways quite different from what we read in Acts. In fact, in the first century there must have been various ways of thinking about the progress of the Christian mission. What if a history had been written that emphasized more the roles of women like Mary Magdalene and Priscilla, for example? We have no evidence that such histories were written, of course, but the mere fact that we can imagine that they could have been highlights my point that Acts is not simply the story of what actually happened. It is selective in what it presents. It follows one stream of events (so that we are not lost on the sea of the myriad things that might have been mentioned).

At the same time, we should note that the picture provided by Acts coheres generally with the New Testament witness as a whole. The book of Acts supports such overall New Testament emphases as the identification of Jesus of Nazareth with the exalted Lord, the continuity between the message of Jesus and that of the early church, and the portrait of the early church as a missionary movement concerned with how the gospel took root and flourished in increasingly Gentile and urban arenas. So my urging that Acts is a historical narrative told from a perspective needs to be read in relation to our awareness that its overall perspective on the early church lines up with what we might call the mainstream of New Testament Christianity.

We recognize today that every statement in a historical work has a documentary as well as an interpretive force. This means that the prevailing view of the last two centuries, that historical inquiry is interested above all in establishing *that* certain events took place and in objectively reporting those "facts," needs to be adjusted somewhat. The primary question is not, How can the past be accurately captured? After all, what events we report and how we report them are always tied to our understanding of what really matters. History-writing interprets the past both by its choice of events to record and by its efforts to show how those events are related in terms of cause and effect. The primary issue becomes, How is the past being represented?

In short, we need to take more seriously than Wesley did the *theological* perspective of the Acts of the Apostles. We need to acknowledge that Luke is interested above all in what God is doing with regard to the birth and mission of the church. We need to grasp how Luke has worked to show us that what happened in the early Christian mission is the result of the empowerment of the Holy Spirit and the guidance of God, and is an expression of nothing less than God's purpose to bring salvation in all its fullness to everyone.

Luke's Book and Wesley's Grace

One of the ways we can see God's hand at work in Acts is to trace what we might call God's choreography of events. Wesley himself did not draw attention to God's hand in this way, but this emphasis is unmistakable to those of us who read Scripture with eyes opened by Wesley's understanding of God's grace at work in the world and of the order of salvation.

One of the hallmarks of Wesley's theology is his understanding of *prevenient grace*. Although Wesley took seriously the Reformation emphasis on the natural sinfulness of all persons, the negative effects of that natural state were for him immediately dampened by his theology of grace—specifically, his understanding of "preventing" or "prevenient" grace. In his sermon "On Working out Our Own Salvation," he wrote:

> Everyone has, sooner or later, good desires; although the generality of men and women stifle them before they can strike deep root, or produce any considerable fruit. Every one has some measure of that light, some faint glimmering ray, which, sooner or later, more or less, enlightens everyone who comes into the world. And every one, unless they be one of the small number whose conscience is seared as with a hot iron, feels more or less uneasy when they act contrary to the light of their own conscience. So no one sins because they have not grace, but because they do not use the grace they have. (§III.4)

This grace is a gift from God to everyone, irrespective of geography or family heritage or merit or status. This is the grace that "goes before," in the sense that God's activity in a person always precedes and enables faithful human response.

The opening of the mission to the Gentiles in the book of Acts is a case study—actually, two case studies—in the exercise of prevenient grace. The first is found in Acts 8:26-40, which narrates the encounter between Philip and the Ethiopian eunuch. From what Luke has written, there is no reason to suspect that this Ethiopian is anything but a Gentile, albeit one who has found in his home country a way to participate on the margins of the Jewish synagogue. He is, like so many others in Acts, a Gentile God-fearer—neither a Jew nor a Gentile proselyte, but one who worships the God of Israel without having actually converted to Judaism. His relationship to Judaism is suggested by two aspects of the story—first, his having come to Jerusalem to worship God (in spite of the fact that, as a eunuch, he could not actually have entered the area of the Temple; see Deut 23:1); and second, his reading a Greek translation of the Scriptures of Israel (that is, the Septuagint).

Note, then, how Luke demonstrates the hand of God at work in this encounter. On a deserted road in the wilderness, we find an Ethiopian eunuch who has made pilgrimage to Jerusalem, like many Gentiles in the ancient world. As he travels down the road, he holds in his hands the scroll of Isaiah and happens to be reading a text (Isa 53:7-8) centered on the humility and exaltation of the Servant of the Lord. For his part, Philip is guided by an angel of the Lord to travel on the same road, then directed by the Holy Spirit to join the eunuch in his chariot (or oxcart).

Narrowing the focus of our telescopic lens, we then see that the Ethiopian eunuch has a question about the text he is reading that Philip is eminently qualified to answer. As they travel together, they happen to find water in this desert place sufficient for the Ethiopian to be baptized, after which Philip is snatched away by the Spirit of the Lord. Think of all the ways the hand of God is at work in this account. Even the translation of Israel's Scriptures into Greek, the worldwide language of the ancient Mediterranean, serves as testimony to the prior work of God that made possible this divine encounter. Consider the ways God was making himself known to the Ethiopian *before* Philip (the evangelist, see Acts 21:8) showed up. Consider, too, the reality that Luke makes no suggestion that the hand of God in this episode overrules the need for human response. If the paths of Philip and the Ethiopian are to intersect around a discussion of Isaiah 53, it is only as they participate with God in responding faithfully to his prior work.

If anything, the story of Cornelius (Acts 10) is even more potent as an example of God's grace at work. Before any encounter with a follower of Christ, a Gentile army officer is known to God for his worship, his providing for the poor, and his prayers. Before any encounter with a follower of Christ, this Gentile has a vision, refers to God as "Lord," and receives assurances from the angel of the Lord. Cornelius and Peter each receive messages from God in visions, both respond faithfully to the instructions they have received, and the result is nothing less than a divine encounter that convinces Peter that "Jesus is Lord of all" and that results in the Spirit's outpouring on Cornelius and his household, as well as their baptism. As with the earlier account of the Ethiopian eunuch, so we find in this one that the landscape of Luke's story is dotted with references to God's gracious hand.

Neither Peter nor Cornelius initiate anything, but both respond faithfully to the initiative of God. Indeed, when criticized for spending time with Cornelius and his household, Peter tells the whole story over again, emphasizing that this was all God's doing (Acts 11:1-18). He concludes, "If then God gave them the same gift that he gave us when we believed in the Lord Jesus Christ, who was I that I could hinder God?" Their response? "When they heard this, they were silenced. And they praised God, saying, 'Then God has given even to the Gentiles the repentance that leads to life'" (11:17-18).

The Book of Acts and the Holy Spirit

So pervasive is the work of God's Spirit in the book of Acts that some have suggested the book ought to be called not "The Acts of the Apostles" but "The Acts of the Holy Spirit." The Spirit is active practically from the first page to the last, with the outpouring of the Spirit at Pentecost fundamental to demonstrating that God had acted decisively to restore his people, that the community of Christ's followers would be a people empowered by the Spirit, and that the church and its mission would be sculpted and directed by the Spirit. Let me mention two aspects of Wesley's interest in the book of Acts that center on the work of the Spirit.

(1) The Spirit at Pentecost. According to Acts 2:1-13, the Spirit fell

upon the gathered followers of Jesus at Pentecost with the result that "all of them were filled with the Holy Spirit and began to speak in other languages, as the Spirit gave them ability" (v. 4). It is easy to imagine that the reason for speaking in other languages was for evangelism, but Wesley saw clearly that the disciples' speech was not so much evangelistic (that is, directed toward those present who were not followers of Jesus) but rather doxological (that is, words of worship, directed toward God). Thus, "in our own languages we hear them speaking about God's deeds of power" (v. 11).

This is important for two reasons. First, as Wesley notes, Acts thus anticipates the day when the praise of God will be heard throughout the world.[3] Thus, the "table of nations" in 2:9-11 is a precursor of the extent of the Christian mission that would follow, to the end of the earth, proclaiming salvation in all its fullness to all people. Second, there is an important sense in which this speaking in other languages was unnecessary at Pentecost, if the purpose of these other languages was evangelistic. This is because everyone present for the Festival of Pentecost—and, in fact, everyone throughout the Roman Empire—would have been able to speak and understand Greek. Greek had become the universal language following Alexander's conquests of what was "the known world" more than three hundred years before the outpouring of the Spirit at Pentecost. This speaking in the languages of these different peoples, then, highlights *both* the universality of the church and its missional reach *and* the fact that what holds the people of God together is not a common language but the one Spirit of God.

The importance of what happens at Pentecost is seen in another of Wesley's emphases, expressed in the response of some Jewish people to these disciples of Jesus in 2:12-13: "All were amazed and perplexed, saying to one another, 'What does this mean?' But others sneered and said, 'They are filled with new wine.' " The inspired speech of the disciples is interpreted by some as nothing but drunken babbling. A similar response to inspired speech occurs in Acts 26:24, the text from which Wesley preached his sermon "The Nature of Enthusiasm." Paul had been allowed to defend himself and the gospel before two Roman officials, Festus and Agrippa. Luke records that "while he was making this defense, Festus exclaimed, 'You are out of your mind, Paul! Too much learning is driving you insane!' " (26:24). Wesley's work with this text follows two different paths. On the one hand, he acknowledges the possibility of an irrational faith, which he attributes to nominal Christians—that is, to people who claim to be Christian but in name only. Of them he writes:

> But the most common of all the enthusiasts of this kind are those who imagine themselves Christians and are not. These abound not only in all parts of our land, but in most parts of the habitable earth. That they are not Christians is clear and undeniable, if we believe the oracles of God. For Christians are holy; these are unholy. Christians love God; these love the world. Christians are humble; these are proud. Christians are gentle; these are passionate. Christians have the mind which was in Christ; these are at the utmost distance from it. Consequently they are no more Christians than they are archangels. Yet they imagine themselves so to be; and they can give several reasons for it. For they have been called so ever since they can remember. They were "christened" many years ago. They embrace the "Christian opinions" vulgarly termed the Christian or catholic faith. They use the "Christian modes of worship," as their ancestors did before them. They live what is called a good "Christian life," as the rest of their neighbors do. And who shall presume to think or say that these people are not Christians? Though without one grain of true faith in Christ, or of real, inward holiness! Without ever having tasted the love of God, or been "made partakers of the Holy Ghost"! (§16)

More to the point of the book of Acts, though, is the other direction Wesley goes, when he admits that, to those whose hearts and minds have been shaped by the patterns of this world, authentic Christians *seem to have lost their minds*. In other words, the reason Festus interrupts Paul's address is not because of Paul's ecstatic or hysterical speech, but rather because of Paul's unexpected exposition of Scripture as witness to Jesus. Lacking the conceptual categories to make sense of Paul's argument, Festus presumes that Paul is the one lacking in intellectual equipment. In both Acts 2 and Acts 26, then, the consequence of Spirit-inspired speech is a charge against the speakers that they had lost their mental capacities. This is not due to their acting like maniacs, but rather because of the strange quality of their proclamation. As Wesley writes, the wonderful things of God proclaimed at Pentecost would have included "the miracles, death, resurrection, and ascension of Christ, together with the effusion of his Spirit, as a fulfillment of his promises, and the glorious dispensations of gospel grace."[4] Attributing all of this to the work of God would make good sense to those who believe that Jesus was sent by God and that these believers had in fact experienced the outpouring of the Spirit. But what about those who did not believe these things? To them it must have seemed at best an enigma and at worst only drunken babbling.

(2) The Spirit and Economic Sharing. Within the Gospel of Luke and Acts of the Apostles, wealth signifies a way of life. Wealth is relational. For this reason, issues of wealth are inescapable for the people of God. This comes into focus in a special way in Luke's characterization of the community of believers in Acts 2:42-47:

> They devoted themselves to the apostles' teaching and fellowship, to the breaking of bread and the prayers.
> Awe came upon everyone, because many wonders and signs were being done by the apostles. All who believed were together and had all things in common; they would sell their possessions and goods and distribute the proceeds to all, as any had need. Day by day, as they spent much time together in the temple, they broke bread at home and ate their food with glad and generous hearts, praising God and having the goodwill of all the people. And day by day the Lord added to their number those who were being saved. (Acts 2:42-47)

Note how "fellowship" is amplified especially in economic terms. This does not mean that fellowship is simply to be *identified* with economic sharing, but that economic sharing is a characteristic and concrete expression of the unity of the believers. As Wesley put it, economic sharing grew out of the great gift of God's grace and out of their love for each other, and was not the result of a command to do so.[5] Those who repented and were baptized are now "those who believe," and their common faith is exhibited materially in economic solidarity. The picture Luke allows is not one of a "common purse," however, nor of disinvestment as a condition for membership into the community. The focus of his presentation falls neither on the ideal of poverty nor on the evil of material possessions nor even on total renunciation as a prerequisite for discipleship. Selling what one has is customary within the community Luke depicts, but such giving is voluntary and is oriented toward addressing the plight of the needy.

Those with ears tuned to the right bandwidth might hear one or more echoes of similar practices or ideals among ancient people: (1) In the Greco-Roman world, it was proverbial that "friends hold all things in common"; in this case, "friends" has been replaced in the well-known proverb with "believers." Luke's portrait is important for its focus on relationships that are defined by egalitarianism and mutuality, not by webs of exchange that turn gifts into a never-ending cycle of repayment and debt. (2) Luke's vision of economic sharing may nourish longings for a utopian "golden age"—a return to the paradise of the Greek's mythic past. Read against this backdrop, Luke's summary might mark a new beginning for humanity. (3) Within the patterns of Palestinian life roughly contemporary with the early Christian community, there are remarkable instances of property sharing among the Jewish people, particularly among the Essenes and at Qumran. These parallels would bring into sharp relief the voluntary character of the economic sharing Luke portrays.

A glance forward to the parallel summary in Acts 4:32-35 is useful. There Luke characterizes practices of economic sharing with language from Deuteronomy 15: "There was not a needy person among them." This was to have been a qualification of those delivered from Egypt, God's people of the exodus. It is now the qualification of God's people of the new exodus.

Wesley has more to say about the character of the authentic church, but what he has to say includes no less than the portrait we find in Acts of this Spirit-generated church in which the grace of God is expressed in economic sharing. In his sermon "The Wisdom of God's Counsels," this is one of the marks of "the glorious church" (§7). And in his sermon "Scriptural Christianity," quoting freely from Acts 2 and 4, he writes of apostolic Christianity:

Such was a Christian in ancient days. Such was every one of those who, "when they heard" the threats of "the chief priests and elders," "lifted up their voice to God with one accord,...and were all filled with the Holy Ghost....The multitude of them that believed were of one heart and of one soul" (so did the love of him in whom they had believed constrain them to love one another). "Neither said any of them that ought of the things which he possessed was his own; but they had all things common." So fully were they crucified to the world and the world crucified to them. "And they continued steadfastly..." "with one accord..." "in the apostles' doctrine, and in the breaking of bread, and in prayers." "And great grace was upon them all; neither was there any among them that lacked: for as many as were possessors of lands or houses sold them, and brought the prices of the things that were sold, and laid them down at the apostles' feet; and distribution was made to all according to their need."

Questions for Reflection and Discussion

1. Acts shows how the church continues the mission of Jesus by widening the circle of God's love to include peoples of all nations. What is your church doing to continue the mission of Jesus? How is your community different because you are there?

2. The church has a missionary mandate, yet many people are uncomfortable about sharing the good news of Jesus Christ. Is this true in your experience? Have you ever been responsible for bringing another person to the love of God?

3. John Wesley wrote a lot about prevenient grace as the freely offered gift of God's love that is present in our lives even before we know God. How was prevenient grace in operation in the life of the Ethiopian eunuch (Acts 8)? In the life of Cornelius (Acts 10)? Share a time when you saw the grace of God at work. Has there been a time in your own life when you have experienced the grace of God?

4. For Wesley, the marks of an authentic church included a Spirit-fueled and inspired community of faith and a fellowship of believers who share with one another, including sharing economic resources. How does your church measure up to Wesley's authentic church criteria? Are there other marks of an authentic church? What are they?

5. When United Methodist pastors prepare for their ordination interview with the Board of Ordained Ministry, they have to answer what it means to say, "Jesus is Lord." If you had to stand up in front of your faith community, what would you say is the meaning of "Jesus is Lord" in your life?

6. In the eyes of the world, a Christian worldview might be considered insane. What is the difference between how a Christian sees the world and how other people might see the world? In terms of the meaning of life, purposeful living, wealth, power, true friendship?

7. In Acts, the Holy Spirit makes the church holy, directs God's people in mission, and empowers God's people for mission. How do you see the Holy Spirit at work in your church? in your life?

6

Romans

> In the evening I went very unwillingly to a society in Aldersgate Street, where someone was reading Luther's Preface to the Epistle to the Romans. About a quarter before nine, while he was describing the change that God works in the heart through faith in Christ, I felt my heart strangely warmed. I felt I did trust in Christ, Christ alone for salvation, and an assurance was given me that he had taken away my sins, even mine, and saved me from the law of sin and death.

So Wesley described the evening of 24 May 1738—known in Methodist lore as his "Aldersgate Experience." In doing so, he bears witness to the importance of Romans for his own formation and assurance as a believer, and hints at the importance this Pauline letter will have for his preaching and theology.

The significant role Paul's letter to the Romans played for Wesley is suggested by the number of sermons he drew from its pages:

- Sermon 5: "Justification by Faith" (Rom 4:5)
- Sermon 6: "The Righteousness of Faith" (Rom 10:5-8)
- Sermon 8: "The First-fruits of the Spirit" (Rom 8:1)
- Sermon 9: "The Spirit of Bondage and of Adoption" (Rom 8:15)
- Sermon 10: "The Witness of the Spirit—Discourse I" (Rom 8:16)
- Sermon 11: "The Witness of the Spirit—Discourse II" (Rom 8:16)

- Sermon 15: "The Great Assize" (Rom 14:10)
- Sermon 17: "The Circumcision of the Heart" (Rom 2:29)
- Sermon 34: "The Original, Nature, Properties, and Use of the Law" (Rom 7:12)
- Sermon 35: "The Law Established through Faith—Discourse I" (Rom 3:31)
- Sermon 36: "The Law Established through Faith—Discourse II" (Rom 3:31)
- Sermon 58: "On Predestination" (Rom 8:29-30)
- Sermon 59: "God's Love to Fallen Man" (Rom 5:15)
- Sermon 60: "The General Deliverance" (Rom 8:19-22)
- Sermon 68: "The Wisdom of God's Counsels" (Rom 11:33)
- Sermon 100: "On Pleasing All Men" (Rom 15:2)
- Sermon 110: "Free Grace" (Rom 8:32)
- Sermon 138B: "On Dissimulation (A Fragment)" (Rom 12:9)

From this list, note especially the importance of Romans 8, a veritable ground zero for a number of characteristic themes of Wesleyan theology, not the least of which is his doctrine of assurance—Wesley's teaching that the Holy Spirit bears witness to people that they are God's children. This theme occupies a central place in his account of his experience on Aldersgate Street, cited above: "an assurance was given me that he had taken away my sins, even mine, and saved me from the law of sin and death." Here he speaks not only of his experience of forgiveness but also of his sense of freedom from the law. This latter point is borrowed from the text of Romans, too: "For the law of the Spirit of life in Christ Jesus has set you free from the law of sin and of death" (Rom 8:2).

The sheer length of his list of discrete sermons is interesting and suggestive, but we see the importance of Romans for Wesley even more clearly in the content of those sermons. Reading his sermon "Justification by Faith," for example, or his two-part series "The Witness of the Spirit," we find ourselves tracking with the heart of Wesley's theology of salvation, his soteriology.

New Testament Letters

Commenting on the movement from the Acts of the Apostles to Romans, Wesley observes that many of the writings of the New Testament are in fact letters. He draws attention to the letters of Paul, James, and Peter, for example, but also to the seven letters comprising Revelation 2–3.[1] Wesley himself was an accomplished letter writer, and he understood how letters written to address a particular question or concern (that is, an "occasional letter") might speak beyond their original situations. Wesley's *Works* include entries from his diaries, pamphlets, and sermons, for example, but also letters. These are not notes dashed off to family or acquaintances, but are often lengthy, sophisticated, and sometimes polemical treatises cast in the form of letters. In this way, they approximate what we find among the New Testament letters—letters written at specific times to specific audiences addressing specific concerns, but with a larger audience in mind. Note, for example, how 2 Corinthians is a letter of Paul to the Corinthians, but its address includes "all the saints throughout Achaia" (2 Cor 1:1)—that is, the Roman province comprising the area we know today as southern Greece. Similarly, toward the end of his letter to the Colossians, Paul gives these instructions: "And when this letter has been read among you, have it read also in the church of the Laodiceans; and see that you read also the letter from Laodicea" (Col 4:16). (We know nothing more about this letter to the Laodiceans.)

In the Roman world of the New Testament era, the importance of letters was linked to the relatively stable nature of the general population. That is, among persons and groups for whom travel from city to city would have been an alien prospect, letters allowed for communication across geographical distance in the absence of any of the myriad forms of more immediate interchange available to us today. Among early Christians, letters were marked by their pastoral origin and destination. They document the early struggle to articulate the concrete character of the gospel in particular settings across the Roman Empire.

The images of "mail" that we might share today are vastly different from those of the first century. First, there was no thought of "dashing off a note." Among some notable authors of letters in the Roman world, the average length of a letter reached as few as 87 words (Cicero, the famous Roman orator [106–43 B.C.]) or as many as 995 (Seneca, the Roman statesman [ca. 4 B.C.–A.D. 65). Compare these figures with the letters of Paul (2,495 words, on average), or the letters of James (about 1,950 words) or 1 Peter (about 1,800 words). The cost of producing even a relatively short New Testament letter—say, James or 1 Peter—would have risen to about $550 in today's economy. Second, relatively few people could actually read. Figures vary, but "literacy," measured in terms of the ability to write and read, would have characterized perhaps 10 percent of the population. Letters were "events," then. Rather than imagining people reading their personal copies of a Pauline letter by the fireplace, we should picture those letters being performed: conveyed to a congregation by someone trained to read interpretively, with gestures and hesitations and voice variations, before an audience of active listeners. We can imagine explanations and questions, give-and-take, as well as repeated performances.

In this way, a letter from Paul functioned like an early version of distance education. They were substitutes for Paul's physical presence, allowing Paul to address questions, deal with problems, and engage in theological formation in spite of the limitations thrust upon him by geographical distance. If "incarnation" refers to "the word made flesh," then these letters can be understood in incarnational terms, as living exemplars of the struggle to bring home the significance of the good news of Jesus Christ in particular times and places.

This is important background for understanding the occasional nature of these New Testament documents. Reflecting on this background also helps us to appreciate the nature of Wesley's theology. From time to time, people will lament the fact that Wesley did not construct for his followers a full-blown systematic theology. Instead, our theological heritage as methodists consists of such materials as sermons, study notes on the New Testament, and pamphlets. This reflects the kind of theologian Wesley was—not so much one lacking in serious reflection on the faith of the church but one whose reflection was tied to the day-to-day realities of an evangelist and preacher. This is a kind of "theology of the streets" (or, thinking of Wesley, we might say, "theology on horseback"). Although others have worked to generate a Wesleyan theological "system,"[2] in the end, to do theology in Wesleyan ways is to bring the resources of our tradition to bear as we critically reflect on the practices of the people of God.

Romans: An "Occasional" Letter?

Wesley thought that Romans was unlike, say, Galatians or 1 Thessalonians. He wrote that Paul seems to write "in a very different manner to those churches that he had planted himself, and to those who had not seen his face in the flesh." In the former letters, Wesley thought, Paul addresses himself in familiar terms—with either loving or sharp words, depending on whether the behavior of his audience had been "suitable to the gospel." When he penned the Letter to the Romans, however, Paul had never been to Rome. Even if his travels had brought him in contact with some Christian believers known among the Romans (see the lengthy list in Romans 16!), he had not founded the church in Rome. Consequently, Wesley thought that, in this letter, Paul "proposes the pure, unmixed gospel, in a more general and abstract manner."[3]

Wesley's characterization of Romans is reminiscent of the words of Melancthon (1497–1560), the early Lutheran theologian. Romans is for him the letter in which Paul "drew up a compendium of Christian doctrine."[4] Although this does not mean for Melancthon that Paul had summarized all aspects of Christian theology (for Romans does not cover some doctrines with much detail or depth), Melancthon does seem to read Romans, like Wesley, as a theological handbook more than as an occasional letter.

For Wesley, the aim of the letter was "to show,

> (1) that neither the Gentiles by the law of nature, nor the Jews by the law of Moses, could obtain justification before God; and that therefore it was necessary for both to seek it from the free mercy of God by faith; and (2) that God has an absolute right to show mercy on what terms he pleases, and to withhold it from those who will not accept it on his own terms.[5]

Wesley's understanding is interesting both for its identifying the importance of justification by faith and for its anticipation of the theme of the vindication of God that we find in more recent study of Romans. Clearly in Romans, Paul identifies trusting in God as the basis for inclusion within the people of God. This, however, is not so much the central argument of Paul's letter as it is the means by which Paul's central emphasis on the universal reach of the good news might be realized in the lives of people, whether Jew or Gentile.

Why did Paul write Romans? The easiest and most straightforward answer to this question is found in Romans 15. Paul finds himself at a juncture in his apostolic ministry. He has "fully proclaimed the good news of Christ" across the vast expanse from Jerusalem to as far around the Mediterranean as the Roman province of Illyricum (located to the northwest of Greece and Macedonia) (Rom 15:19). He does not want to cover the ground where other missionaries have gone before him, but has made it his ambition to proclaim the good news to the west, from Italy and onto Spain (Rom 15:20-24). He sees Rome as the base camp from which to launch his missionary expedition; he anticipates both staying with them for a while en route to Spain and their sending him eastward with their support (Rom 1:13; 15:24). Paul's aim in writing Romans, then, was to establish a relationship with these believers and to secure their material support.

If this is the easiest and most straightforward answer to why Paul wrote this letter, it is also not altogether satisfying. After all, Paul did not need to write what would become the longest and most theologically dense of his New Testament letters in order to achieve this end. Obviously, Romans is more than a fund-raising letter! In fact, additional evidence from the opening and concluding chapters of the letter suggests that Paul used the opportunity of this letter to address issues of concern among the Roman Christians, too. This allowed him to articulate key aspects of the gospel message in a way that took seriously the situation of house churches in Rome. In A.D. 49, six to eight years before Paul's letter, the Roman emperor Claudius had expelled Jews from Rome after a debate among the Roman Jews concerning the identity and role of Christ (see Acts 18:2). The result would have been house churches dominated by Gentiles. About five years later, when Jews returned to Rome after Claudius's death, the relationship between Jews and Gentiles within the church would have become a flashpoint.

A single verse in the final chapter of Romans helps to communicate what Paul attempts in this profound letter: "Greet one another with a holy kiss" (Rom 16:16). Wesley wrote about this verse, "So the ancient Christians concluded all their solemn offices: the men saluting the men, and the women the women."[6] No evidence supports this last interpretation—that is, that women and men did not exchange the "holy kiss"—but it is easy enough to see why Wesley might have introduced it, so as to stave off potential erotic practices among followers of Christ. In fact, in the Greco-Roman world, the erotic significance of kissing, particularly public kissing, was at best secondary. Kissing was for relatives, for greeting, parting, concluding contracts, and to signal reconciliation (see, e.g., Luke 7:45; Acts 20:37-38). Paul qualifies the kiss as "holy." On the one hand, this means simply that these kisses belong to God.

On the other, and more to the point in this context, the holy kiss signifies the forging of relationships within the church, crossing the boundaries that separate people from one another. That Paul instructs the Romans to practice the holy kiss (the verb is in the imperative) means that we must not assume that this practice was already (or merely) customary. Divisions were present and they needed to be traversed and overcome.

In this setting, then, the holy kiss was a visible expression of the unity of the people of God. It was the gospel in action. In the case of the Romans to whom Paul has addressed this letter, the holy kiss put into practice a gospel message that brought the two together, Jew and Gentile, as an organic unity, in mutual acceptance, across social and religious lines, negating observance of differences of status. It meant treating others as if they were members of one's own extended network of family relationships. As one commentator has put it, "The holy kiss overcomes shameful discrimination and celebrates the glorious freedom of the children of God."[7]

Wesley and Romans

Among the many ways Wesley read Romans, let me mention two—one that may be surprising to contemporary followers of Wesley, and one that strikes more recognizably at the heart of his thought.

(1) Animals and the New Creation. In his sermon "The General Deliverance" (based on Rom 8:19-22), Wesley developed what was at the time an extraordinary link between humanity and animals, a link that must be understood under the more general umbrella of an emphasis on God's redeeming purposes for physical creation. Wesley was an avid reader in the natural sciences and he attempted in various ways to integrate scientific understanding with scriptural knowledge. He was influenced by the 1764 publication of T. Hartley's *Paradise Restored,* which had examined biblical support for the idea that the age of salvation would include all of creation. He also knew T. Burnet's *The Sacred Theory of the Earth* (1684/1690), an early attempt to integrate biblical portraits of creation, the flood, and the new heavens and new earth with emerging scientific discovery. Indeed, in a journal entry of 17 January 1770, Wesley documents his judgment that Burnet's views were "highly probable." Unlike Burnet, though, Wesley thought that the new creation was God's act permanently to reform and improve the created order.

In "The General Deliverance," Wesley recognized how close human beings were to the animal world. Speaking of the original state of things at creation, and with reference to animals as "brutes," he wrote:

> What then makes the barrier between humanity and brutes? The line which they cannot pass? It was not reason. Set aside that ambiguous term: exchange it for the plain word, understanding, and who can deny that brutes have this? We may as well deny that they have sight or hearing. But it is this: humanity is capable of God; the inferior creatures are not. We have no ground to believe that they are in any degree capable of knowing, loving, or obeying God. (§I.5)

Together with the inanimate world, animals shared in the results of the fall of humanity into sin. Consequently, "Well might the apostle say of this, 'The whole creation groans together, and travails together in pain until now.' This directly refers to the brute creation" (§I.6, citing Rom 8:22).

> What, then, will happen at the restoration of all things?
> The whole brute creation will then undoubtedly be restored, not only to the vigor, strength, and swiftness they had at their creation, but to a far higher degree of each than they ever enjoyed. They will be restored, not only to that measure of understanding which they had in paradise, but to a degree of it as much higher than that as the understanding of an elephant is beyond that of a worm. And whatever affections they had in the garden of God will be restored with vast increase, being exalted and refined in a manner that we ourselves are not now able to comprehend. The liberty they then had will be completely restored, and they will be free in all their motions. They will be delivered from all irregular appetites, from all unruly passions, from every disposition that is either evil in itself or has any tendency to evil. No rage will be found in any creature, no fierceness, no cruelty or thirst for blood. So far from it that "the wolf shall dwell with the lamb, the leopard shall lie down with the kid, the calf and the young lion together; and a little child shall lead them. The cow and the bear shall feed together, and the lion shall eat straw like the ox. . . . They shall not hurt or destroy in all my holy mountain." (§III.3)

Actually, Wesley takes this vision of God's good ends even further. He speculates,

> What if it should then please the all-wise, the all-gracious Creator, to raise them higher in the scale of beings? What if it should please him, when he makes us "equal to angels," to make them what we are now? Creatures capable of God? Capable of knowing, and loving, and enjoying the Author of their being? . . . However this be, he will certainly do what will be most for his own glory. (§III.6)

Clearly, for Wesley, the inclusion of animals in the new creation was not a minor question, but was grounded in our affirmation of God's graciousness and glory. His interests are motivated further by what it might mean to speak of the restoration of all creation—

and how God's affirmation of creation at the end of time ought to direct human attitudes and behaviors on behalf of creation today.

(2) Justification by Faith. "How a sinner may be justified before God, the Lord and Judge of all, is a question of no common importance to every person. It contains the foundation of all our hope, inasmuch as while we are at enmity with God there can be no true peace, no solid joy, either in time or in eternity." With these words, John Wesley opens his sermon on Romans 4:5, "Justification by Faith." And with these words he testifies to the absolute centrality of this doctrine to his understanding of Christian faith and life. In this sermon, he proposes to answer four questions: Why is justification needed? What is justification? Who is justified? On what terms are they justified?

First, why is justification needed? Taking what is for Wesley a well-worn road, Wesley observes that humanity was created in God's image: "By the free, unmerited love of God the human was holy and happy; the human knew, loved, enjoyed God, which is (in substance) life everlasting. And in this life of love humanity was to continue forever if they would continue to obey God in all things" (§I.4). But this is precisely what they did not do. "By the sin of the first Adam, who was not only the ancestor but likewise the representative of us all, we all 'fell short of the favor of God'" (§I.9).

Second, what is justification? Wesley defines justification in part by saying what it is not. Thus, for example, justification should not be confused with its fruit, sanctification. Justification has to do with "what God *does for us* through his Son," whereas sanctification describes "what he *works in us* by his Spirit" (§II.1). Nor is justification an act of deception, whereby God thinks that we are something other than what we are. That is, in justification, God is not fooled into thinking that we are somehow without sin, or that we were somehow made righteous apart from his grace. Rather, "the plain scriptural notion of justification is pardon, the forgiveness of sins" (§II.4).

Third, who is justified? On this point, Wesley could hardly be more straightforward. "It is only sinners that have any occasion for pardon: it is sin alone that admits of being forgiven" (§III.1). This emphasis is developed elsewhere in the words of Paul himself:

For while we were still weak, at the right time Christ died for the ungodly. Indeed, rarely will anyone die for a righteous person—though perhaps for a good person someone might actually dare to die. But God proves his love for us in that while we still were sinners Christ died for us. Much more surely then, now that we have been justified by his blood, will we be saved through him from the wrath of God. For if while we were enemies, we were reconciled to God through the death of his Son, much more surely, having been reconciled, will we be saved by his life. (Rom 5:6-10)

Finally, on what terms are they justified? There is only one condition of justification, and this is faith. Without faith, there is no justification. Nothing other than faith is necessary for justification. Although faith is a human response to the grace of God, faith is not of human origin. Justifying faith, rather, is also the gift of God.

Against the backdrop of Wesley's understanding of justification by faith, a few words of clarification are in order. This is because it is easy for us in the English-speaking world to hear legal overtones in the language of justification, as though Paul were portraying God as a judge pronouncing "not guilty" over sinful humans and so freeing them from the punishment they deserve on account of their failings. The background of Paul's thought was not the courtroom per se, but God's covenantal relationship with Israel. "Justification" in this context refers to being in right relationship with God. That is, the primary metaphor is relational rather than legal. This means that the general outline of Wesley's view of justification needs to be read within the grand mural of God's covenant faithfulness, rather than in terms borrowed from English (or American) courts of law.

"Sin," then, is not simply "breaking the law" or "wrongdoing," but a failure on the part of humans to live in covenant relationship with God. This rebellion takes several forms, especially forms of idolatry (see Rom 1:18-32), leading persons away from loving God and loving their neighbors. Accordingly, the death of Jesus puts on display God's covenant faithfulness both to forgive people of their sin and to deliver them from the power of sin. When Paul calls on humans to place their trust in God, through the saving work of God's Son, he calls on them to leave behind their attitudes and behaviors of rebellion against God. What is more, he calls on them to declare their allegiance to their new Lord, and to act in ways that reflect the will of God as this was demonstrated in the faithful life and sacrificial death of Jesus. For Paul, then, the death of Jesus is central to justification both because it makes forgiveness possible and because it demonstrates the nature of faithful life in the world.

Perhaps not surprisingly, Wesley closes his sermon "Justification by Faith" with a call for response:

> You who are ungodly, who hear or read these words, you vile, helpless, miserable sinner, I charge you before God, the judge of all, go straight to him with all your ungodliness. Take heed that you do not destroy your own soul by pleading your righteousness, more or less. Go as altogether ungodly, guilty, lost, destroyed, deserving and dropping into hell, and you shall then find favor in his sight, and know that he justifies the ungodly.... You who feel you art just fit for hell are just fit to advance his glory: the glory of his free grace.... Come quickly. Believe in the Lord Jesus; and you, even you, are reconciled to God. (§IV.9)

Questions for Reflection and Discussion

1. The book of Romans was of special and personal interest to John Wesley. What is your favorite book of the Bible or favorite Scripture passage? Why? What does it say about your faith journey?

2. Romans is a letter written by Paul. A letter is a particular form of communication. How does a letter differ from other forms of communication? a newspaper editorial? a blog? an e-mail? a Twitter post? an essay? a report? a newsletter?

3. For Wesley the saving grace of God through Jesus Christ means that we can be justified before God. Because we are justified we enter into a right relationship with God. What does being in a right relationship with God mean to you? What are the characteristics of a right relationship with God? with another person?

4. We are justified by faith alone, not by conforming to laws, rituals, or decrees. Through our faith we receive pardon of our sins and are enabled to enter into God's glorious kingdom. How can

faith be strengthened? How does faith begin to take shape in a person's life? How can others see where you put your faith? Reflect on a time when your faith was tested.

5. Wesley believed that God's love extends to all people no matter what one's social position or status. God's love even extends to animals. If God loves all creation, how are we to act as God's representatives? Are we called up to treat creation in particular ways?

6. Our faith is anchored in the hope as seen in the life, death, and resurrection of Jesus Christ. In what or whom do you place your hope? Where do you see faith, hope, and love in your life and in the life of your church? Where should you see faith, hope, and love? Whom do you know who exemplifies faithful and hopeful living?

7
1–2 Corinthians

Paul's correspondence with the Corinthians stands in sharp contrast with his Letter to the Romans. Wesley's reference to Romans as a "general and abstract" presentation of the gospel would make no sense as a description of 1 or 2 Corinthians. Here we find some of Paul's most personal correspondence, documenting something of the lengthy and complicated story of the relationship between Paul and the Corinthian Christians.

According to Acts 18, Paul had lived among the Corinthians some eighteen months, founding the Corinthian church and providing leadership during its infancy. What motivated this lengthy commitment? Three reasons come to mind. (1) First, Paul found immediate lodging and work, and subsequent monetary support for this lengthy, initial stage of his mission. Luke writes that, when Paul came to Corinth,

> there he found a Jew named Aquila, a native of Pontus, who had recently come from Italy with his wife Priscilla, because Claudius had ordered all Jews to leave Rome. Paul went to see them, and, because he was of the same trade, he stayed with them, and they worked together—by trade they were tentmakers. (Acts 18:2-3)

Although the narrative of Acts does not say so, other texts suggest that, when Timothy and Silas traveled from Macedonia to join Paul in Corinth, they brought monetary support so that Paul was able to curtail his daily schedule as a leather-worker, allowing him more time for preaching and teaching (see Acts 18:5;

2 Cor 11:8-9; Phil 4:15). In other words, a number of circumstances aligned so as to provide Paul a convenient setting for the work of evangelism and church-planting.

(2) Additionally, Corinth was an eminently strategic city for the spread of the good news. The city was located in the Roman province of Achaia, where it commanded the isthmus between the Greek north and south. What is more, it held two harbors, from which it commanded the premier sea route from Rome in the west to the eastern Mediterranean. As Strabo, the Roman geographer put it, "Corinth is called 'wealthy' because of its commerce, since it is situated on the Isthmus and is master of two harbors, of which the one leads straight to Asia, and the other to Italy" (*Geography* 8.6.20). With traffic between north and south, east and west, required to pass through Corinth, the city developed as a commercial, political, military, and religious center and crossroads.

Wesley was very much aware of the significance of Corinth's location, and opened his comments on 1 Corinthians by observing an important corollary:

> Corinth was a city of Achaia, situated on the isthmus that joins Peloponnesus, now called the Morea, to the rest of Greece. Being so advantageously situated for trade, the inhabitants of it abounded in riches, which, by too natural a consequence, led them into luxury, lewdness, and all manner of vice.[1]

Indeed, Cicero (106–43 B.C.) wrote that "maritime cities also suggest a certain corruption and degeneration of morals; for they receive a mixture of strange languages and customs, and import foreign ways as well as foreign merchandise, so that none of their ancestral institutions can possibly remain unchanged" (*On the Republic*, 2.7–9). When we recall that Corinth's strategic location had led to its destruction by Rome in 146 B.C., only to be rebuilt in 44 B.C., the importance of Cicero's observation is highlighted all the more. This is because the city Paul visited and made his temporary home was relatively young and had few ancestral traditions to provide it with a moral compass in the first place. In fact, Corinth's luxury and vice had led earlier to the coining of the Greek term, *korinthiazomai*, which might be translated "to act like a Corinthian"—or, more fully, "to behave immorally," or even "to fornicate." Clearly Corinth was a difficult place for a Christian community.

(3) A third reason why Paul lived among the Corinthian believers for such a lengthy time must have been the nature of the city and its population, which presented special challenges for founding and forming a Christian community. The people of Corinth had no ancestral narrative to speak of and few built-in restraints on their behavior. The challenge for Paul, then, was to show this predominately Gentile church its real roots in the story of Israel and to induct them into the ways of the crucified Christ.

Wesley wrote that 1 Corinthians "concerned the affairs of the Corinthians," whereas in 2 Corinthians Paul was more concerned with himself.[2] There is some truth to this. In 1 Corinthians, Paul has received reports about divisions among the Corinthians (see 1 Cor 1:11) as well as a letter from the Corinthians raising various questions about the nature of faithful living (see 1 Cor 7:1; 8:1; 12:1). In 2 Corinthians, though, the nature of the relationship between Paul and the Corinthian believers has deteriorated to such a degree that he needed to undertake a defense of his apostleship, which is really a defense of the gospel itself. In spite of these differences, the center of Paul's message remains the same in both letters. Whether calling Corinthian behavior into question, urging their participation in a collection he is raising for the believers in Jerusalem, scolding his opponents, or documenting the nature of his apostolic service, Paul's message centers on the cross of Christ. Indeed, he writes, "I decided to know nothing among you except Jesus Christ, and him crucified" (1 Cor 2:2)—not because he spoke of nothing but the crucified Christ among the Corinthians, but because the entirety of his message had as its hub the cross of Christ. Christ crucified is not only the basis of salvation but also the measure of their discipleship and his apostleship. They were to follow in the footsteps of their crucified Lord by putting into play in their daily lives the faithfulness and orientation to the other on display in the cross.

Wesley and Paul's Corinthian Correspondence

A number of Wesley's sermons are grounded in texts found in 1–2 Corinthians:

- Sermon 12: "The Witness of Our Own Spirit" (2 Cor 1:12)
- Sermon 13: "On Sin in Believers" (2 Cor 5:17)
- Sermon 41: "Wandering Thoughts" (2 Cor 10:4)
- Sermon 42: "Satan's Devices" (2 Cor 2:11)
- Sermon 69: "The Imperfection of Human Knowledge" (1 Cor 13:9)
- Sermon 70: "The Case of Reason Impartially Considered" (1 Cor 14:20)
- Sermon 75: "On Schism" (1 Cor 12:25)
- Sermon 79: "On Dissipation" (1 Cor 7:35)
- Sermon 81: "In What Sense We Are to Leave the World" (2 Cor 6:17-18)
- Sermon 82: "On Temptation" (1 Cor 10:13)
- Sermon 89: "The More Excellent Way" (1 Cor 12:31)
- Sermon 91: "On Charity" (1 Cor 13:1-3)
- Sermon 105: "On Conscience" (2 Cor 1:12)
- Sermon 119: "Walking by Sight and Walking by Faith" (2 Cor 5:7)
- Sermon 123: "On Knowing Christ after the Flesh" (2 Cor 5:16)
- Sermon 129: "Heavenly Treasure in Earthen Vessels" (2 Cor 4:7)
- Sermon 137: "On Corrupting the Word of God" (2 Cor 2:17)
- Sermon 149: "On Love" (1 Cor 13:3)[3]

How can we explain this extensive interest in Paul's letters to the Corinthians? Undoubtedly, Wesley was drawn to 1 and 2 Corinthians in large part because these letters brought so fully to the surface in the New Testament the kinds of issues that were so important to those in Wesley's evangelical movement in the eighteenth century. I refer to the presence of temptation and sin among believers and, then, to how Wesley might best articulate his understanding of that pivotal Wesleyan doctrine of Christian perfection.

In his teaching on Christian perfection, Wesley seemed often to engage in a rear-guard action, as much denying what Christian perfection was not as affirming as what it was. Apparently, this was a doctrine that attracted misunderstanding. So, for example, Christian perfection does not refer to a state of Christian maturity beyond which one could mature no further. Christian perfection does not refer to a status from which the believer might not experience a failure of faith and, so, fall back into sin. Christian perfection did not signify that a believer was perfect in knowledge. Given typical understandings of "perfection," Wesley's denial of "sinless perfection" is perhaps his most important qualification of his emphasis on holiness of heart and life.

It was this last point that is so important to our reading of Wesley as an interpreter of 1–2 Corinthians. Notice how Paul addresses the Corinthian believers in the salutation of his first letter: "those who are sanctified in Christ Jesus" and "called to be saints" (1 Cor 1:2). Paul thus emphasizes God's initiative both in making believers holy and in calling them to be holy. In doing so, though, he leaves open the question to what degree they are actually living out their holiness in everyday life.

Wesley's sermon on 2 Corinthians 5:17 is aptly titled "On Sin in Believers." Note at the outset the difference in these three translations:

- "Therefore if any man be in Christ, *he is a new creature*: old things are passed away; behold, all things are become new."
- "Therefore if any one be in Christ, *there is a new creation*: the old things are passed away; behold, all things are become new."
- "So if anyone is in Christ, *there is a new creation*: everything old has passed away; see, everything has become new!"

I have italicized the key difference among them. The first is the Authorized Version, what we commonly call the King James Version, prevalent in Wesley's day and generally his preferred translation. The second, though, is Wesley's own translation. That is, it represents Wesley's correction of the Authorized Version.[4] The third comes from the NRSV. Anticipating the NRSV, Wesley's alteration of the Authorized Version begins to take seriously Paul's concern not simply with "individual change," but with a radical reorientation of the whole of life in relation to God's work of renewing all things. Wesley's gloss on the first phrase, "if any one be in Christ," is simply this: "A true believer in him [that is, in Christ]." His note on the second phrase, "there is a new creation," is more interesting: "God, humanity, heaven, earth, and all therein, appear in a new light, and stand related to the believer in a new manner, since the believer was created anew in Christ Jesus."[5]

How does he explain this change in his sermon? First, Wesley introduces the problem, which was in fact much debated in his time.

> Is there then sin in those that are in Christ? Does sin remain in one that "believes in him"? Is there any sin in them that are "born of God," or are they wholly delivered from it? Let no one imagine this to be a question of mere curiosity, or that it is of little importance whether it be determined one way or the other. Rather it is a point of the utmost moment to all serious Christians, the resolving of which very nearly concerns both their present and eternal happiness. (§I.1)

Wesley responds at length, then, to explain how it is that believers might have undergone the radical change of which Paul speaks in 2 Corinthians 5:17 *and* yet sin. In doing so, he first makes a strong case that this is actually the nature of things, that true Christians might sin—and this is where the Corinthian context of his sermon comes especially into play.

In an earlier sermon, "The Mystery of Iniquity," Wesley observed of the believers at Corinth, "But how early did the mystery of iniquity work, and how powerfully, in the church at Corinth! Not only 'schisms' and 'heresies,' animosities, fierce and bitter contentions were among them, but open, actual sins; indeed, 'such fornication as was not named among the heathens.' " What is more, Paul needed to remind the Corinthian believers that " 'neither adulterers, nor thieves, nor drunkards' could 'enter into the kingdom of heaven.' " Alluding to the parable of the weeds sown among the wheat in Matthew 13:24-30, Wesley continues, "And in all St. Paul's epistles we meet with abundant proof that weeds grew up with the wheat in all the churches, and that the mystery of iniquity did everywhere in a thousand forms work against the mystery of godliness" (§18).

Similarly, in his sermon "On Sin in Believers," he observes of Paul:

> When he writes to the believers at Corinth, to those who were "sanctified in Christ Jesus," Paul says, "I, brethren, could not speak unto you as unto spiritual, but as unto carnal, as unto babes in Christ. . . . You are yet carnal: for whereas there is among you envying and strife, . . . are you not carnal?" Now here the apostle speaks to those who were unquestionably believers, whom in the same breath he styles his "brothers and sisters in Christ," as being still in a measure carnal.

By "carnal," Paul refers to "behavior stemming from human rather than godly desires." In the case of the text Wesley is citing, 1 Corinthians 3:1-3, those desires are expressed in terms of divisions and rivalries within the church. As Wesley goes on to observe,

> He affirms there was "envying" (an evil temper) occasioning "strife" among them, and yet does not give the least intimation that they had lost their faith. No, he manifestly declares they had not; for then they would not have been "babes in Christ." And (what is most remarkable of all) he speaks of being "carnal" and "babes in Christ" as one and the same thing; plainly showing that every believer is (in a degree) "carnal" while he or she is only a "babe in Christ."

Wesley draws from the evidence of Paul's letter—indeed, from all of Paul's letters and the whole of Scripture—"that there are two contrary principles in believers—nature and grace, the flesh and the spirit." What is more, for Wesley almost everything Paul has to say to his churches is grounded in this fact, that wrong dispositions and behaviors continue among those who have been born anew. Thus, believers "are continually exhorted to fight with and conquer these, by the power of the faith that was in them" (§III.2–3).

From this Wesley reasserts his claim against those who might say that there is no sin among those who have been justified.

Actually, he rests his case on a four-legged stool. The teaching that believers, from the moment they are justified, are without sin:

- is contrary to the whole witness of Scripture,
- is contrary to the experience of God's children,
- is contrary to the early tradition of the church (and is therefore nothing but a new teaching that must for this reason be rejected), and
- causes true believers to despair and even lose the faith, since their experience runs counter to this teaching.

What, then, does it mean to say, with Paul, that, "if any one be in Christ, there is a new creation"? Wesley writes:

> We must not so interpret the apostle's words as to make him contradict himself. And if we will make him consistent with himself the plain meaning of the words is this: the believer's *old judgment* (concerning justification, holiness, happiness, indeed concerning the things of God in general) is now "passed away"; so are those *old desires, designs, affections, tempers,* and *conversation*. All these are undeniably "become new," greatly changed from what they were. And yet, though they are *new,* they are not *wholly* new. (§IV.2)

To put it more succinctly, Wesley now articulates the believer's relationship to sin in almost proverbial fashion: "The believer is saved from sin; yet not entirely: it *remains,* though it does not *reign*" (§IV.3). Taking the sermon as a whole, we can push further in articulating how Wesley understands sin in relation to the believer. For him, the *guilt* of sin is addressed in justification and the *power* of sin is undercut in God's act of new creation, so that the *reality* of sin is removed in the sanctifying of the believer.

First-Century Corinthians and Eighteenth-Century Methodists

Wesley's work with 1–2 Corinthians invites us to reflect further on the nature of his theological interpretation of Scripture. It may be easiest to get a handle on what he has done by comparing it with how the Bible has come to be read by many since Wesley's day.

For many trained in biblical interpretation in modern times, biblical interpretation would be seen as a two-stage process. First we find what a biblical text meant in its own time and place; then, on the basis of what the Bible meant, we ask how that meaning might be expressed today. We move from "what it meant" to "what it means." Sometimes, this approach has more than two stages, but the effect is much the same. For example, one might move, step-by-step, from *observation* to *interpretation,* and then from *interpretation* to *application.* Here, too, the "application" of the text typically takes the form of a translation of the text into principles that can then be applied (or made relevant) to today.

Note carefully what this approach to biblical interpretation assumes. Moving from "what it meant" to "what it means" presumes that a biblical text is a document grounded in its historical past, separated from us by the great chasm of time. Accordingly, a letter like 1 Corinthians is irrelevant to contemporary faith and life until it is transformed in some way. That is, it needs to be made "applicable." On the surface, this way of thinking about reading the Bible probably makes sense. After all, 1 Corinthians was written to the Corinthians in the mid-first century. We live in a different time and place, so if the ancient message of Paul is to have any significance for us today, this significance (or "application") will come if and only if we allow the text to speak to its original audience in its original time and then try to tease out principles from the text that we might apply to our own time.

This is a helpful approach insofar as it requires us to slow down as we read the text. It appropriately reminds us that the Corinthians were not eighteenth-century British Methodists, or twenty-first-century Americans, as though they shared the concerns and values and interests that we take for granted. In a sense, then, two-stage biblical interpretation "protects" the biblical text from us, from our attempts to remake the biblical text in our own image. It is true: human tendencies toward pride, self-sufficiency, and self-autonomy lead us to think that everything is about us. So we easily come to these texts asking a single question, What does it mean to me? We need to allow the text its own voice.

Notice, though, that the two-stage reading of the Bible assumes that the Bible is first and foremost a historical document. By this

I mean that this way of reading the Bible assumes that the meaning of a biblical text is focused on that ancient time and place when the text was written. And it assumes that what separates us from a text like 1 Corinthians is history. The Bible has its history. We have our history. The Corinthians lived in their own time and place. We live in a different time and place. These claims follow naturally from the notion that the Bible is a historical document. Does this way of reading the Bible do justice, though, to our understanding of the Bible as Christian Scripture, as the book by which we shape our common faith and life as Christians?

Notice, too, that Wesley did not work with this two-stage approach to reading 1–2 Corinthians. His sermons on 1 Corinthians do not first establish what Paul must have meant in the first century so that Wesley can then add a section to his sermon entitled "How 1 Corinthians Applies to Us" or "The Relevance of 1 Corinthians for Today." But neither did he imagine that 1 Corinthians had been written in the eighteenth century, as though it were written to address the theological arguments and everyday concerns of the Methodist movement.

Instead, Wesley came to the text aware *both* of his theological questions and commitments *and* of the origins of 1 Corinthians within the ongoing relationship between the apostle Paul and the Corinthian Christians. Instead, Wesley comes to the text with the working assumption that, as Scripture, 1 Corinthians was written not only for a first-century audience but for eighteenth-century Christians as well.

Writing in 1 Corinthians of the Old Testament story of the exodus journey, Paul had observed, "These things happened to them to serve as an example, and they were written down to instruct us, on whom the ends of the ages have come" (1 Cor 10:11). It is as if Wesley had said the same of 1 Corinthians: "These things were written to serve as an example to us, and to instruct us...."

Thus, Wesley could say that the Scriptures teach the same thing that our Christian experience has shown us. This is that the same people whom God has made holy, the same people whom God has called to be "saints"—these same people can at the same time live according to sinful desires. It is as if Wesley might say, "Those Corinthians...they are us and we are them." The result is that what Paul says of the Corinthians he also says of the people called Methodists. Of course Wesley understands that there are differences between first-century Corinth and eighteenth-century England. His notes on 1 Corinthians make this clear enough. But he moves forward with his reading of the text anyway, taking seriously that the social and historical differences between the Corinthian Christians and the Methodist Christians do not take away from the theological similarities that bind together those Corinthians and these Methodists. To push further, we might say that Wesley works to lay bare the situation among the Corinthians so that Methodists can see themselves in the text, so that they can hear its message as if it were their own.

What is the difference between the two approaches we have sketched? Wesley does not work this out as fully as he might have. This is perhaps due largely to the fact that he read the Bible the way he did according to his own, well-developed theological intuitions, rather than as the result of a carefully worked-out theory of interpretation. Nevertheless, the difference is plain. *The two-stage approach* to biblical interpretation assumes that the message of 1 Corinthians is located in a first-century historical moment; hence, if 1 Corinthians is going to speak to us, it will be as we transform that message into twenty-first-century terms. *Wesley's approach* starts in a different place. If 1 Corinthians is Scripture, then its significance is certainly shaped by but never limited to that first-century context.

What is needed is not a transformation of the meaning of the Bible, but a transformation of those who hear the Bible. Subsequent readers of 1 Corinthians, like Wesley or like you and me, need to find our way into the text so that we identify with its readers as sinner-saints. When we do, our tendencies toward division and rivalry are exposed and we hear its crystal clear call to live lives before God and with each other that are determined by the self-giving of the cross of Christ.

Questions for Reflection and Discussion

1. Ancient Corinth was a cosmopolitan city with ties well beyond where it was geographically located. How does this compare with

where you live? How do your surroundings affect you—the traffic, distance you have to travel on a daily basis, available venues for learning, sports, and entertainment, even shopping? How do your surroundings affect how you can practice your faith?

2. Like Jesus and like the Corinthians, temptations confront us. How do you deal with temptation? What resources does your faith provide to help you face your temptations? What is a good course of action to take when a person is helpless to fight temptation?

3. Wesley said that even Christians sin, but that even though sin remains it does not rule our lives. What is the difference?

4. Some people accuse the church of being full of hypocrites. Needless to say, that is true; but it does not have to be the final word about church people. How should Christians respond to the charge of being hypocritical—saying one thing, but doing another?

5. When artists draw an image that looks exactly like the thing drawn, they say that drawing is closely rendered. In other words, the drawing is a faithful representation. How closely does your church reflect the life and teachings of Christ? What steps can your church take to become a more faithful rendering of Christ? What steps do you need to take personally?

6. As Christians we are new creations in Christ and thus are radically transformed and reformed into the image of Christ. What does this mean for your daily living? How do you need to change?

7. Wesley's way of understanding the Bible suggests that reading it is meant to transform our lives, because through it, God can grab our attention, help us, and shower us with grace. How has your Bible reading changed you? Are the spiritual gifts of love, joy, peace, patience, kindness, generosity, faithfulness, gentleness, and self-control more evident in your life than they were a year ago? six months ago? last week? yesterday?

8. Too many churches (and too many people) are rent with division, rivalry, and even general negativity. What does this say about their spiritual health? What can you do to help your church respond more faithfully to the call of God to be loving and self-giving?

8
Hebrews

After the Gospel of Matthew, the letter to the Hebrews is the biblical book from which Wesley preached most often. Albert Outler counted 965 occasions on which Wesley turned to Hebrews for his text.[1] What Wesley seems not to have said explicitly is why this is so.

Concerning the purpose of Hebrews, Wesley wrote:

> The scope of it is to confirm their faith in Christ; and this the author does by demonstrating the glory of Christ. All the parts of it are full of the most earnest and pointed admonitions and exhortations; and they go on in one tenor, the particle *therefore* everywhere connecting the doctrine and the use.[2]

With these words, Wesley observes that the author of Hebrews devotes much of the letter to Christology. The author repeatedly interrupts this teaching about Christ in order to show its immediate consequences for the lives of believers. This is what Wesley means when he writes that "the particle *therefore*" connects "the doctrine and the use." Wesley might have taken a further step, though. He might have observed how transparently the argument of Hebrews puts on display what is clearly central to Wesley's theology—namely, the journey of salvation. For Hebrews as for Wesley, salvation was not merely a fixed point in the past but an ongoing pilgrimage as one moves forward to maturity in the faith.

Hebrews calls itself a "word of exhortation" (Heb 13:22). The same phrase is used in Acts 13:15 of a sermon or homily, suggesting that Hebrews should be read as a written sermon. Its aim is to encourage the fidelity or faithfulness of believers against the temptation to leave the faith in the midst of trials. Hebrews 3:12-14 is one of several points at which the author steps away from his larger teaching about Christ in order to urge believers onward:

> Take care, brothers and sisters, that none of you may have an evil, unbelieving heart that turns away from the living God. But exhort one another every day, as long as it is called "today," so that none of you may be hardened by the deceitfulness of sin. For we have become partners of Christ, if only we hold our first confidence firm to the end.

With this passage, we can compare others, including Hebrews 2:1-3; 3:1; 4:1-2, 11-16; 5:11–6:12; 10:19-39; 12:1-28. These demonstrate that believers are like people living in exile, for whom the struggles of minority existence and pressures to conform to the values and behaviors of the wider world provide a constant motivation to fall away from the faith. Within the argument of the letter as a whole, though, these words of encouragement show that believers have the necessary resources for continuing in the faith. They have God's own self-revelation, they are cleansed from their sins, they have a Savior who has opened for them the path of salvation and who now leads them on that path, they share in the Holy Spirit, they are empowered to set aside whatever constraints keep them from moving on, they have numerous persons who have gone on before as exemplars of faithfulness, they have enumerated for them certain Christian practices that encourage ongoing faithfulness, and, not insignificantly, they have each other as traveling companions.

Though Wesley preached from Hebrews repeatedly, the number of sermons available to us is few:

- Sermon 71: "Of Good Angels" (Heb 1:14)
- Sermon 76: "On Perfection" (Heb 6:1)
- Sermon 97: "On Obedience to Pastors" (Heb 13:17)
- Sermon 106: "On Faith" (Heb 11:6)
- Sermon 117: "On the Discoveries of Faith (Heb 11:1)
- Sermon 121: "Prophets and Priests" (Heb 5:4)
- Sermon 132: "On Faith" (Heb 11:1)

Going on to Perfection

According to Albert Outler's calculations, between 1739 and 1785 Wesley preached from Hebrews 6:1 fifty times. The text itself comprises a turning point in a larger section of the letter, 5:11–6:12:

> About this we have much to say that is hard to explain, since you have become dull in understanding. For though by this time you ought to be teachers, you need someone to teach you again the basic elements of the oracles of God. You need milk, not solid food; for everyone who lives on milk, being still an infant, is unskilled in the word of righteousness. But solid food is for the mature, for those whose faculties have been trained by practice to distinguish good from evil.
>
> Therefore let us go on toward perfection, leaving behind the basic teaching about Christ, and not laying again the foundation: repentance from dead works and faith toward God, instruction about baptisms, laying on of hands, resurrection of the dead, and eternal judgment. And we will do this, if God permits. For it is impossible to restore again to repentance those who have once been enlightened, and have tasted the heavenly gift, and have shared in the Holy Spirit, and have tasted the goodness of the word of God and the powers of the age to come, and then have fallen away, since on their own they are crucifying again the Son of God and are holding him up to contempt. Ground that drinks up the rain falling on it repeatedly, and that produces a crop useful to those for whom it is cultivated, receives a blessing from God. But if it produces thorns and thistles, it is worthless and on the verge of being cursed; its end is to be burned over.
>
> Even though we speak in this way, beloved, we are confident of better things in your case, things that belong to salvation. For God is not unjust; he will not overlook your work and the love that you showed for his sake in serving the saints, as you still do. And we want each one of you to show the same diligence so as to realize the full assurance of hope to the very end, so that you may not become sluggish, but imitators of those who through faith and patience inherit the promises.

On one level, the sense of this larger text is clear enough. In these verses, the author has taken leave of his lengthy exposition of the nature of the priesthood of Christ Jesus in order to call upon his audience to move on in the pilgrimage of discipleship. We can see something of the irony of the situation the author faces in the arrangement of 5:11–6:3:

A		They need to be taught the basics (5:11-13)
	B	They should be mature (5:14)
	B'	They need to go on to maturity (NRSV: "perfection") (6:1a)
A'		They need to move beyond the basics (6:1-3)

From irony, the author turns to urgency in 6:4-8: a menacing warning about falling away.

Read against the backdrop of the whole letter, we find other resonances. Wesley observes of Hebrews that it is concerned with two overarching comparisons: "(1) The prophets, the angels, Moses, Joshua, Aaron, are great; but Jesus Christ is infinitely greater. (2) The ancient believers enjoyed high privileges; but Christian believers enjoy far higher."[3] From the perspective of Hebrews, one of the shortcomings of Israel's faith as this is set out in the Old Testament is that its means for addressing sin—namely, the priesthood and sacrifices—were incapable of leading persons on to the desired goal of perfection. This problem is overcome by Jesus Christ in two ways. First, he is both the perfect priest and the perfect sacrifice, so that his self-offering dealt with human sinfulness once and for all. Second, as Hebrews 12:2 clarifies, Jesus is the leader or pioneer of human salvation. He opens the path and leads his followers on the journey of perfect faithfulness. What does "perfection" mean in this context? Certainly, Hebrews is concerned with moral goodness, with doing good, but this is not the whole story. This is because Jesus, though he was "holy, blameless, undefiled, separated from sinners, and exalted above the heavens" (Heb 7:26), had still to become perfect (Heb 2:10; 5:7-9; 7:28). "Perfect," then, has to do not only with Jesus' character, dispositions, and allegiances but also with his embracing faithfully the path set before him by God. Jesus thus walked faithfully the path of obedience to God *and* blazed the trail of holy living that others might follow.

Wesley's notes on 6:1 encapsulate a key theological insight.

Weaving his comments into the text of Hebrews, he writes, "*And this we will do*—We will go on to perfection; and so much the more diligently, because, *It is impossible for those who were once enlightened.*"[4] On the one hand, Wesley is confident in the grace of God that empowers believers to move on toward perfection. On the other, he is clear that believers, once they have experienced the new birth, have no choice other than to move on toward perfection. *Moving on in the journey of salvation is nonnegotiable. Not to move on is to fall away.*

Wesley's sermon "On Perfection" begins with just this emphasis, noting that it is just "as if the author had said, 'If we do not "go on to perfection," we are in the utmost danger of "falling away." And if we do fall away, it is "impossible" (that is, exceedingly hard) "to renew them again unto repentance." ' " Before moving on, we should observe that Wesley has not only, yet again, underscored the importance of moving forward in Christian faithfulness. He has also interpreted the *impossibility* of restoring those who have left the faith as *possible*, though "exceedingly hard." Although in making this interpretive move he takes us outside Hebrews, he nevertheless finds reason to do so in Jesus' words to his disciples in Matthew's Gospel regarding the salvation of the wealthy: "For mortals it is impossible, but for God all things are possible" (Matt 19:26). This is consistent with Wesley's view of the universality of grace—the gift of grace available to all persons, and thus the possibility that any person, empowered by God's gift of grace, might yet respond to God in faith.

The purpose of the sermon, though, lies elsewhere. He wants above all to show what "perfection" is. As we have come to expect when Wesley turns to the question of Christian perfection, he begins by saying what it is not. It is not "the perfection of angels." Humans have chosen the way of sin whereas angels have not, and it is impossible for humans in this life to achieve again what was lost on account of sin. With regard to angels, though, Wesley says that "their affections are all constantly guided by their unerring understanding, so all their actions are suitable thereto; so they do every moment not their own will but the good and acceptable will of God" (§I.1). For the same reason, Christian perfection is not the achievement of the purity of Adam and Eve in their initial paradisal state. Having given in to sin, "humankind is no longer able to avoid falling into innumerable mistakes; consequently humans cannot always avoid wrong affections; neither can they always think, speak, and act right" (§I.2).

Nor does perfection exclude ignorance and error. Wesley admits:

> Now from wrong judgments wrong words and actions will often necessarily flow. And in some cases wrong affections also may spring from the same source. I may judge wrong of you: I may think more or less highly of you than I ought to think. And this mistake in my judgment may not only occasion something wrong in my behavior, but it may have a still deeper effect—it may occasion something wrong in my affection. From a wrong apprehension I may love and esteem you either more or less than I ought. (§I.3)

Thus, for every person, and at every moment of a person's life, there is need of the atoning death of Christ by which God reconciles the world to himself.

What, then, is Christian perfection? Wesley begins a lengthy digest of biblical texts with this definition:

> It is the complying with that kind command, "My child, give me your heart." It is the "loving the Lord your God with all your heart, and with all your soul, and with all your mind." This is the sum of Christian perfection: it is all comprised in that one word, love. The first branch of it is the love of God: and as those who love God love their brothers and sisters also, it is inseparably connected with the second, "You will love your neighbor as yourself." Thou shalt love everyone as you love your own soul, as Christ loved us. "On these two commandments hang all the law and the prophets": these contain the whole of Christian perfection. (§1.4)

From here, Wesley takes his audience on a veritable tour of New Testament letters, citing passages from Philippians, Galatians, Ephesians, 1 Peter, 1 Thessalonians, and Romans in an effort to explain the heart and soul of Christian perfection. These can be summarized in words borrowed from the Old Testament: love God with all that you are and love your neighbor as yourself (Deut 6:5; Lev 19:18).

Nowhere in this sermon, though, does Wesley turn to Hebrews itself in order to make sense of the term he has found in Hebrews 6:1, "perfection." What are we to make of this? It is worth noting that the author of Hebrews has not helped us much at this point. On the basis of the language of 6:1 itself, we cannot fill in much of the content of this term. We do have some hints, though. In a way more transparent in the Greek text than in English translations, the author uses words with roots denoting the "beginning" (*arch-*) and "end" (*tel-*). This comports well with Wesley's interest in moving on in the faith. And it reminds us of Wesley's understanding of new birth according to the biological analogy of growth from infancy to adulthood. The idea of maturation toward a goal is developed further in verses 9-12:

> Even though we speak in this way, beloved, we are confident of better things in your case, things that belong to salvation. For God is not unjust; he will not overlook your work and the love that you showed for his sake in serving the saints, as you still do. And we want each one of you to show the same diligence so as to realize the full assurance of hope to the very end, so that you may not become sluggish, but imitators of those who through faith and patience inherit the promises.

From here, we see how the language of perfection corresponds to achieving "things that belong to salvation," acts of love and service among the saints, realizing "the full assurance of hope to the very end," and, ultimately, inheriting the promises. These emphases assume that the death of Jesus cleanses believers of sin *and* propels believers on in their fellowship with God and other believers.

Students of the Bible often learn to rehearse this mantra, "Context! Context! Context!" That is, texts must be interpreted in context. Today, students of the Bible typically learn to identify "context" both as "literary context" and as "historical context." Accordingly, we should ask concerning "perfection" in Hebrews 6:1: (1) What role does "perfection" play in the Letter to the Hebrews? How does Hebrews 5:11–6:12 help us to discern the meaning of "perfection" in 6:1? (2) How would the first audience of Hebrews understand the word *perfection*? Would they think of the use of the term in ancient philosophy? In Israel's Scriptures? And so on.

It would be wrong to imagine that Wesley did not also learn the same mantra, "Context!" But this is not to say that Wesley parsed the idea of "context" in the same way that we teach and learn today in formal biblical studies. He reads the phrase "going on to perfection" within a context—this is obvious. But by "context" he means *not only* literary or historical context *but also* "the whole tenor of Scripture." Thus, we should view the author of Hebrew's encouragement to go on to perfection within the context of the teaching of the whole of Scripture regarding the journey of salvation. The notion of Christian perfection, then, is set within Wesley's doctrine of salvation. And we can fill out the meaning of "perfection" by ranging across the whole of Scripture, wherever we find phrases that explain what God is after in divine-human relations, wherever we find phrases that explain the ends for which God entered into human history to redeem us in Christ:

- "Let the same mind be in you that was in Christ Jesus" (Phil 2:5).
- "The fruit of the Spirit is love, joy, peace, patience, kindness, generosity, faithfulness, gentleness, and self-control" (Gal 5:22-23).
- "Like obedient children, do not be conformed to the desires that you formerly had in ignorance. Instead, as he who called you is holy, be holy yourselves in all your conduct; for it is written, 'You shall be holy, for I am holy'" (1 Pet 1:14-16).

And on the list goes. In this way, we see that Wesley reads Scripture with this aim in mind: to nurture love of God and love of neighbor. In the end, this is the theological context within which he practices biblical interpretation.

Attending upon All the Ordinances of God

At the outset of the passage in Hebrews that runs from 5:11 to 6:12, the writer addresses an underlying problem of his audience. They have become "dull in understanding" (5:11). It is easy to miss the nuance of this phrase when it is rendered into English in this way. The writer actually begins and ends this larger section with the same term, "lazy" (*nōthros* in Greek, translated by the NRSV as "dull" in 5:11 and as "sluggish" in 6:12). In other words, the writer charges his audience with inactivity—their sitting alongside the road rather than progressing along it, we might say. Their lack of progress in the pilgrimage of faith is tied to their need for practical action.

We can grasp better the importance of the way the author has thus framed this section by reflecting on the organic relationship between dispositions (what Wesley called "tempers") and practices. By "dispositions," I refer to attitudes, inclinations, and allegiances—one's patterns of thinking, believing, and feeling. By "practices," I refer to patterns of behavior in which people engage that are oriented toward their formation in the service of a goal intrinsic to the practice itself. Taken together, these patterns of thinking, feeling, believing, and behaving comprise our formation as persons. We can visualize the relationship between dispositions and practices as follows:

Dispositions

↓ ↑

Practices

The point, of course, is this: dispositions give rise to practices, but our practices help to sculpt our dispositions. As Wesley reported in a journal entry of 5 March 1738, during Wesley's own crisis of faith Peter Böhler had urged him, "Preach faith *till* you have it, and then, *because* you have it, you *will* preach faith."

The perspective of Hebrews is that certain practices must not be neglected, in spite of strong reasons to do so. The writer of Hebrews is particularly sensitive to the suffering of his audience, a suffering that undoubtedly arises from the struggles of living as a minority people—that is, as Christians—within the larger world. This is alien life, life lived against the grain of the social, political, and religious conventions regarded as normal and good by those who do not follow Christ. The pressure to conform is strong, so that baby-steps toward accommodation easily give way to giant strides toward falling away altogether. In the face of such pressures, certain Christian practices serve as both prophylactic and antidote. Christians engage in such practices because of their allegiance to Christ, and their engagement in those practices forms them more fully in their allegiance to Christ.

What are these practices? Hebrews identifies certain Christian practices as integral to progressing on the journey of salvation (see, for example, 3:12-13; 4:1; 6:10; 10:24-25; 12:15-16; 13:1-3). Some examples:

- Watching over one another in mutual accountability, support, and encouragement
- Performing acts of love and service toward other believers
- Challenging each other to perform acts of love and good deeds
- Assembling together, presumably for shared meals and encouragement
- Hospitality toward strangers

To add one or two more strokes to the portrait we are painting here, let me refer to some of Hebrew's final words: "We have an altar from which those who officiate in the tent have no right to eat.... Through him, then, let us continually offer a sacrifice of praise to God, that is, the fruit of lips that confess his name. Do not neglect to do good and to share what you have, for such sacrifices are pleasing to God" (13:10, 15-16). This reference to an altar assumes the legislation in Leviticus 24:5-9 regarding what priests alone were allowed to eat—a reference that our author now turns on its head by naming an altar at which priests could not eat. What is this "Christian altar"? Wesley understood it as a reference to the "cross of Christ."[5] This is surely correct, though it is also difficult to avoid thoughts of the Lord's Supper—which recalls the cross of Christ, the saving benefits of Jesus' death, and the eucharistic call to live lives that honor Jesus' self-offering on the cross. In Hebrews 13:15-16, the writer goes further to identify worship of God, doing good, and sharing what one has as sacrifices pleasing to God. These are nothing less than the natural outgrowths of the lives of believers who are progressing on the journey of salvation, but they also propel these believers farther down the path.

Although there is no one-to-one overlap between the teaching of Hebrews and the persistent position of John Wesley, there is nonetheless strong coherence at this crucial point: Christians engage in certain practices because of their allegiance to Christ, and their engagement in those practices forms them more fully in their allegiance to Christ. Faithfulness of heart and faithfulness of life are symbiotic, the one forever nurturing the other. What practices does Wesley emphasize?

In his booklet concerning the "Nature, Design, and Rules of the United Societies," Wesley sets out, first, the entrance requirement for admission to these preaching meetings. "There is one only condition previously required in those who desire admission into these societies, a desire 'to flee from the wrath to come, to be saved from their sins.'" In order to continue in these meetings, however, persons needed not only to claim but also to demonstrate this desire. "It is therefore expected of all who continue therein, that they should continue to evidence their desire of salvation." The nature of this evidence Wesley summarized under three headings:

- First, by doing no harm
- Second, by doing good
- Third, by attending upon all the ordinances of God

It is this third expectation, "attending upon all the ordinances of God," to which I draw attention here, since these are reminiscent of a key element of the direction given by the Letter to the Hebrews.

Wesley refers to these "ordinances," which he also enumerates as "means of grace," in various places. A list would include:

- The public worship of God
- The ministry of the word, either read or expounded
- The Lord's Supper
- Family and private prayer
- Searching the Scriptures (which implies reading, hearing, and meditating on the Scriptures)
- Fasting, or abstinence

Through such means as these, Wesley acknowledges in his sermon "The More Excellent Way," the higher order of Christians "spared no pains to arrive at the summit of Christian holiness; 'leaving the first principles of the doctrine of Christ, to go on to perfection'; to 'know all that love of God that passes knowledge, and to be filled with all the fulness of God'" (§6). The astute reader will recognize that he has quoted from Hebrews 6:1, tying the "ordinances of God" to the pilgrimage of Christian maturity advocated by the author of Hebrews.

What is more, Wesley himself devised a network of small groups, the purpose of which tracks significantly with the concerns we have found in Hebrews. The United Society was "a company of people having the form and seeking the power of godliness, united in order to pray together, to receive the word of exhortation, and to watch over one another in love, that they may help each other to work out their salvation."[6] These were adjunct to the worship services of the Anglican Church, and were preaching services structured for group discipleship. The crowning glory of Wesley's organization, though, was the class meeting, which provided for weekly meetings of lay-pastoral oversight, mutual accountability, and encouragement. In "A Plain Account of the People Called Methodists," Wesley observes the result:

> Many now happily experienced that Christian fellowship of which they had not so much as an idea before. They began to "bear one another's burdens," and naturally to "care for each other." As they had daily a more intimate acquaintance with, so they had a more endeared affection for, each other. And "speaking the truth in love, they grew up into him in all things, who is the Head, even Christ." (§II.7)

Wesley is sometimes criticized for focusing too much on the salvation of the individual. But emphases like these underscore his recognition that Christian life is a community affair, that the journey of salvation is a group project. Mutual care requires Christian community, and failure to travel together is a sign of a lag in faithfulness. As the author of Hebrews puts it, "Let us consider how to provoke one another to love and good deeds, not neglecting to meet together, as is the habit of some, but encouraging one another, and all the more as you see the Day approaching" (10:24-25).

Questions for Reflection and Discussion

1. Hebrews was an important book for Wesley because it helped him understand the nature and significance of Jesus. Read the book of Hebrews for yourself. What passages speak to you?
2. The spiritual life is a journey into the heart of God. What appeals to you most about being on, what Wesley called, the road to perfection?
3. What does it mean to love God with all your heart, soul, mind, and strength? How can you give more to God? How can the Holy Spirit help you?
4. Who we are as persons affects what we do, our practices. But our practices also shape who we are as persons. The relation between who we are and our practices is reciprocal. How does your daily living affect who you are spiritually?
5. Wesley says that if we are not journeying toward God, we have fallen away. In other words, if we are not moving toward God, we are moving away from God. Where are you? Are you moving toward God or away from God? Where is your church?
6. As Christians we are to outdo each other in doing good. In other words, we are called to compete with each other in acts of love and service. If your church was handing out awards, where would you place? In your opinion, who are the front runners?
7. How do you and your church rate when it comes to watching over each other in accountability, support, and encouragement; performing acts of love and service; challenging each other to perform acts of love and good deeds; assembling together for worship and fellowship; and being hospitable toward strangers? Rate your church on a scale of one to ten for each of these, one being low and ten being high. How does your church encourage these practices?
8. Wesley was a big believer in and the founder of many small groups. How can being in a small group help you on your Christian walk? Are you currently in such a group? What would you need to have such a group?

9

James and 1 Peter

The letters of James and 1 Peter have this in common: both are addressed to folks who are not at home, who do not belong, folks whose lives are lived on the margins of acceptable society, whose deepest allegiances and dispositions do not line up very well with what matters most in the world in which they live. Thus, 1 Peter is addressed "to the exiles of the Dispersion" (1:1), and the Letter of James "to the twelve tribes in the Dispersion" (1:1).

Dispersion, exile—running through a register of terms brought to mind, we might entertain images of trauma, expulsion from the homeland, violence, life on the move—away from usual social programs and infrastructure, erosion of identity, movement from the center to the periphery of the comfortable and the valued, loss of social and cultural roots, torn from the nourishment of family and tradition, refugees. Here is a register of the sorts of terms James and 1 Peter use to portray the situation of their respective audiences:

James	1 Peter
"trials of any kind" (1:2)	"tested by fire" (1:7)
the "testing of your faith" (1:3)	abused (2:23; 3:9)
humiliation (1:9)	suffering (2:23)
"temptation" (1:12)	reviled (3:16)
"distress" (1:27)	slandered (3:16)
"conflicts and disputes" (4:1)	"reviled for the name of Christ" (4:14)
victims of fraudulent behavior (5:4)	suffering as a Christian (4:16)

condemnation and murder (5:6)
a life of "wandering" (5:20)

In their own ways, then, James and 1 Peter concern themselves pointedly with the life-situation most Christians face in the world today. The Christian movement is a minority movement within the wider world. This is true even in so-called Christian countries—that is, where a majority of the population self-identify as Christians—since it is one thing to identify oneself as a "Christian" and quite another to risk minority status through the risky identification of oneself with that same redemptive work of God that resulted in the crucifixion of God's own Son. How ought Christians live in the midst of wider social currents that do not honor Jesus as Lord of the whole of life?

Life in Exile

As further backdrop for understanding what is at stake in these two books, James and 1 Peter, we can reflect briefly on three of the primary realities of life "in exile."

First, exile refers to an in-between time and an in-between place. The life of the exile is a particularly vulnerable one. Exiles live between memories of home and the freedom that comes with stability on the one hand, and hopes of restoration on the other.

Second, exile is a time of identity formation. Living at home and among our own people, we think little of what makes us who we are: our idioms, our typical practices, the foods we eat, our habits or work and play, the taken-for-granted conventions by which we know who we are. Living among others, such questions demand fresh attention. Who are *we* in relation to *them*? What is the basis of *our* constitution as a community? What are *our* characteristic practices? By what strategies do we keep faith with who we are? It is, then, no small thing when Daniel, that faithful exile, seems willing enough to be taught the language and literature of the Chaldeans, yet "resolved that he would not defile himself with the royal rations of food and wine" (Dan 1:8).

Third, exile is a time of temptation and testing. The experience of exile resides in this: the social and religious threat confronting

120

a people challenged with the perennial possibility and threat of assimilation and defection. James refers to this as the problem of *peirasmos*—a Greek term that can be translated both as "testing" and as "temptation." The paradox, which we find in both James and 1 Peter, is that the very process that can lead to growth in faith and faithfulness toward God (that is, "testing") can also lead to loss of faithfulness, even falling away from faith (that is, "temptation").

Given Wesley's heightened interests in the process of maturation as a disciple of Christ and in personal and social holiness, we have good reason to ask what he made of these two letters, whose concerns were so much his own.

Wesley and James

We have two sermons from Wesley on the Letter of James:

- Sermon 80: "On Friendship with the World" (Jas 4:4)
- Sermon 83: "On Patience" (Jas 1:4)

Actually, that second sermon is less "On Patience" and more "On Perfection." In Wesley's slightly edited text of the Authorized Version, James 1:4 reads, "But let patience have its perfect work, that you may be perfect and entire, wanting nothing."[1] Not surprisingly, it is the second clause, "that you may be perfect," that attracts Wesley's attention. This is clear throughout, but especially as the sermon reaches its climactic, final paragraph:

> You shall then be perfect. James seems to mean by this expression, *teleioi,* you shall be wholly delivered from every evil work, from every evil word, from every sinful thought; indeed, from every evil desire, passion, temper, from all inbred corruption, from all remains of the carnal mind, from the whole body of sin: and you shall be renewed in the spirit of your mind, in every right temper, after the image of him that created you, in righteousness and true holiness. (§14)

How is this perfection achieved? Within his sermon, Wesley debates whether perfection is gradual or instantaneous. Does it happen in a moment or is it the result of a process? Twice, he concludes that this is not the most important issue. He insists, rather, that whether "perfection" is experienced instantaneously or gradually, this "change" is a gift from God and we must never rest until this change is ours. This dual emphasis on God's initiative and human cooperation with God through perseverance is typical of our tradition as methodists.

James, we may recall, is focused here on how followers of Christ live in the context of the struggle. As a result, he lays out a process with one of two possible outcomes. When believers face trials of various kinds, they should respond in the right way, with joy. This is the progression in James 1:2-4:

trials → endurance → maturation (or perfection)

However, there is a counterprogression in James 1:14-15:

temptation → sin → death

I have already observed that the term for "trial" and "temptation" in Greek is the same. The question arises, then: when is a trial really a temptation (and vice versa)? For James, the answer seems clear enough. A difficult life experience can be either a trial or a temptation, depending on the believer's response to it. It is a "trial" (that leads to maturation) when believers respond to it appropriately, with joy; but it is a "temptation" (that leads to death) when believers respond to it inappropriately, out of their own evil inclinations. In other words, believers cannot blame their outward circumstances for their lack of Christian growth or for failures of faith. (Nor can they blame God—see James 1:13.) The gracious God has given them the wherewithal needed not only for surviving in difficult circumstances, but for flourishing in their faith. Commenting on this progression in James, Wesley himself concluded, "We are therefore to look for the cause of every sin, *in*, not *out of*, ourselves."[2]

James develops this process in a slightly different way later in the chapter, when he sets human "desire" or "craving" or even "evil inclinations" in contrast with God's "desire" or "will" (see Jas 1:14-15, 18, 21). Accordingly:

122

God's desire,	Human desire
by means of the "word of truth" or the "implanted word,"	
gives us birth "so that we would become a kind of first fruits of his creatures."	gives birth to sin and sin gives birth to death.

In this chain of cause-and-effect, we see that the gospel itself (the "word of truth") is powerful when it is internalized (as the "implanted word") in the lives of those who follow Christ.

Elsewhere, James diagnoses the situation in different terms, though with the same results. He writes, "Adulterers! Do you not know that friendship with the world is enmity with God? Therefore whoever wishes to be a friend of the world becomes an enemy of God" (Jas 4:4). The importance of this text is grounded in ancient ideas about "friendship," understood among ancient philosophers in terms of the unity of heart and mind shared among friends. Cicero (106–43 B.C.) described friendship as "nothing other than the agreement over all things divine and human along with good will and affection" (*De amic.* 6.20). What would it mean, then, to have "friendship with the world"? In a famous text, the Gospel of John reports Jesus' words, "God so loved the world..." (John 3:16). James uses the term "world" quite differently. His concern is not with the extent of God's graciousness toward the world (though he does think in these terms), but rather with the unrelenting negative response of the world to God. So he uses the term "world" negatively again and again in this short letter (see Jas 1:27; 2:5; 3:6; 4:4).

Insight into "friendship with the world" can be found in a number of texts in James's letter, but perhaps nowhere more clearly than in his depiction of "earthly" wisdom in terms of "bitter envy and selfish ambition in your hearts," which gives rise to "disorder and wickedness of every kind" (3:14-16). This is the opposite of the wisdom God gives, which "is first pure, then peaceable, gentle, willing to yield, full of mercy and good fruits, without a trace of partiality or hypocrisy" (3:17; see 1:5). Along these same lines, when James labels his audience as "adulterers" (4:4), he calls to mind the biblical tradition of Israel as God's unfaithful spouse. It is as if those having (or claiming) an exclusive, covenant relationship with Yahweh are also participating in idolatry. Simply put, no one can have unity of heart and mind with God *and* also with the world.

Apparently, Wesley was concerned that church folk in his own day were friends of the world, with the result that the other sermon on James that we have from his hand is on this text in James. In "On Friendship with the World," he claims that there are "very few subjects of so deep importance; few that so nearly concern the very essence of religion" (§1). Even Methodists, he observes, have been affected by the negative consequences of this friendship with the world.

> For want of understanding this advice of the Apostle (I hope, rather than from any contempt of it) many among them are sick, spiritually sick, and many sleep who were once thoroughly awakened. And it is well if they awake any more till their souls are required of them. It has appeared difficult to me to account for what I have frequently observed: many who were once greatly alive to God, whose conversation was in heaven, who had their affections on things above, not on things of the earth; though they walked in all the ordinances of God, though they still abounded in good works, and abstained from all known sin, yes, and from the appearance of evil; yet they gradually and insensibly decayed . . . insomuch that they are less alive to God now than they were ten, twenty, or thirty years ago. But it is easily accounted for if we observe that as they increased in goods they increased in "friendship with the world," which indeed must always be the case unless the mighty power of God interpose. (§3)

As he often does, Wesley organizes his sermon around questions. First, what does James mean by "world"? On this, Wesley reaches a pithy conclusion: "Fix in your heart this plain meaning of the term 'the world'—those who do not fear God. Let no one deceive you with vain words: it means neither more nor less than this" (§7). Second, he questions what sort of acquaintance Christians might have with the world. After all, he admits, we cannot withdraw from the world or abandon the object of God's grace.

We may, we ought to love them as ourselves (for they also are in-cluded in the word "neighbor"); to bear them real goodwill; to desire their happiness as sincerely as we desire our own happi-ness; indeed, we are in a sense to honor them (seeing we are di-rected by the apostle to "honor all people") as the creatures of God. (§8)

He continues,

We may doubtless converse with them, first, on business, in the various purposes of this life, according to that station therein, wherein the providence of God has placed us; secondly, when courtesy requires it—only we must take great care not to carry it too far; thirdly, when we have a reasonable hope of doing them good. (§10)

We should notice that the shape of Wesley's sermon is deter-mined by transformations in the meaning of "friendship." What is true in the classical world, that "friendship" was understood above all in ideal terms of intimacy of heart and life, was no longer true in Wesley's Britain in the eighteenth century. Nor is it true in our own world of "social networking" and lengthy lists of friends. This means that Wesley's sermon moves into a level of practicality even further than this most practical of New Testa-ment letters, James! This is especially true in the next stage of his sermon, where Wesley begins to get at the heart of what he re-gards as inappropriate expressions of friendship.

Third, then, Wesley reaches the primary question: What friend-ship must we not have with the world? He begins by observing that "we may easily hurt our own souls by sliding into a close attach-ment to any of them that know not God. This is the 'friendship' that is 'enmity with God': we cannot be too jealous over ourselves, lest we fall into this deadly snare; lest we contract, or ever we are aware, a love of complacence or delight in them" (§11). His parade exam-ple of wrong "friendship with the world" is the marriage between a person who follows Christ and one who does not.

Above all, we should tremble at the very thought of entering into a marriage covenant, the closest of all others, with any per-son who does not love, or at least, fear God. This is the most horrid folly, the most deplorable madness, that a child of God can possibly plunge into, as it implies every sort of connection with the ungodly which a Christian is bound in conscience to avoid. No wonder then it is so flatly forbidden of God; that the prohibition is so absolute and peremptory: "Be not unequally yoked with an unbeliever." (§12)

Fourth, Wesley inquires, Why is friendship with the world forbidden? He provides two answers: (1) such friendship is a sin in itself, since friendship with the world is nothing less than "spiritual idolatry" (§13); and (2) because of the deadly consequences of such friendship, which he describes at length in terms that are reminiscent of James's own thoughts concerning human cravings, desires, and evil inclinations. Using the language of hunting and fishing, James has it that one's cravings set a trap, they bait and hook—they lure and entice (Jas 1:14). This, Wesley would underscore, is the consequence of befriending the world.

Wesley ends this impassioned sermon with a plea to the people called Methodists:

> But whatever others do, whether they will hear or whether they will forbear, hear this, all ye that are called Methodists. However much you are urged or tempted, have no friendship with the world. Look round and see the melancholy effects it has produced among your brothers and sisters! How many of the mighty are fallen! How many have fallen by this very thing! They would take no warning: they would converse, and that intimately, with earthly minded people....O "come out from among them," from all unholy persons, however harmless they may appear, "and separate yourselves"!—at least so far as to have no intimacy with them. As "your fellowship is with the Father, and with his Son Jesus Christ," so let it be with those, and those only, who at least seek the Lord Jesus Christ in sincerity. So "shall you be," in a peculiar sense, "my sons and my daughters, saith the Lord Almighty." (§28)

Wesley and 1 Peter

"There is a wonderful weightiness, and yet liveliness and sweetness, in the epistles of St. Peter." With these words, Wesley introduces 1–2 Peter.[3] Though his diary is peppered with references to both letters, they are the basis of only two sermons we have from Wesley's hand, both from texts in 1 Peter:

- Sermon 46: "Heaviness through Manifold Temptations" (1 Pet 1:6)
- Sermon 88: "On Dress" (1 Pet 3:3-4)

"On Dress" makes for interesting reading not so much as an interpretation of 1 Peter, but as a case study in how Wesley has dropped the words of 1 Peter into the laps of his eighteenth-century Methodist churches. First, Peter's words:

> Do not adorn yourselves outwardly by braiding your hair, and by wearing gold ornaments or fine clothing; rather, let your adornment be the inner self with the lasting beauty of a gentle and quiet spirit, which is very precious in God's sight. (1 Pet 3:3-4)

In the first-century Roman world, the world of Peter and his audience, a person *was* his or her clothing—that is, what one wore put on display one's character, one's status in the community. As a result, all sorts of first-century documents, including legal materials and philosophical writings, concerned themselves with proper dress. Writing in the mid-first century, Seneca (ca. 4 B.C.–A.D. 65) praised his mother with these words:

> Unchastity, the greatest evil of our time, has never classed you with the great majority of women. Jewels have not moved you, nor pearls. . . . You have never defiled your face with paints and cosmetics. Never have you fancied the kind of dress that exposed no greater nakedness by being removed. Your only ornament, the kind of beauty that time does not tarnish, is the great honor of modesty. (*Ad Helv.* 16.3–5)

Accordingly, the items that Peter lists—braiding of hair, gold, and fine clothing—would have been regarded as windows into a woman's essential self. In Peter's world, such clothing would have paraded for all to see such character qualities as lack of self-control, immodesty, snootiness, even sensuality. Set over against eye-catching fashion is a "hidden" heart that pleases God.

Without taking its audience on a guided tour of eye-catching fashion on the streets of first-century Asia Minor, Wesley's sermon performs a similar task. After affirming neatness of dress and overall good grooming, Wesley answers the question, What do we display by our fine clothes and costly jewelry? Here begins an annotated list of problems:

- It breeds pride, for "nothing is more natural than to think ourselves better because we are dressed in better clothes" (§9).
- It cultivates vanity—that is, "the love and desire of being admired and praised" (§11).
- It leads naturally to anger—which Wesley regards as the opposite of the attitudes championed by Peter: "a gentle and quiet spirit, which is very precious in God's sight" (1 Pet 3:4).
- It inflames lust, a word Wesley uses apparently to convey the idea that costly apparel arouses sexual desire.
- It is contrary to wearing the clothing (so to speak) of good works: "every shilling you needlessly spend on your apparel is in effect stolen from God and the poor" (§14).
- It is contrary to concerning oneself foremost with the inner heart. "All the time you are studying this 'outward adorning,' the whole inward work of the Spirit stands still; or rather goes back, though by very gentle and almost imperceptible degrees. Instead of growing more heavenly-minded, you are more and more earthly-minded" (§19).

Wesley concludes his list with these words: "All these evils, and a thousand more, spring from that one root—indulging yourself in costly apparel" (§19). Instead, drawing on the language of Paul, followers of Christ ought to "put on Christ" (see Rom 13:14; Gal 3:27). Listen to Wesley's words as he turns even more directly to address methodist Christians:

> I call upon you all who have any regard for me, show me before I go hence that I have not labored, even in this respect, in vain

for near half a century. Let me see, before I die, a Methodist congregation full as plain dressed as a Quaker congregation. Only be more consistent with yourselves. Let your dress be cheap as well as plain. Otherwise you do but trifle with God and me, and your own souls. I pray, let there be no costly silks among you, how grave soever they may be. Let there be no *Quaker-linen*, proverbially so called for their exquisite fineness; no Brussels lace, no elephantine hats or bonnets, those scandals of female modesty. Be all of a piece, dressed from head to foot as persons "professing godliness"; professing to do everything small and great with the single view of pleasing God. (§26)

Wesley on Predestination

The opening of Peter's letter is important for the way it identifies the character of Peter's target audience. It is also interesting for the space it opens up for Wesley to discuss one of the more debated theological questions of his day. The text reads as follows:

> Peter, apostle of Jesus Christ, to the chosen, strangers in the world of the diaspora in Pontus, Galatia, Cappadocia, Asia, and Bithynia, according to the foreknowledge of God the Father, in the sanctification of the Spirit, because of the obedience and sprinkling of the blood of Jesus Christ: May grace and peace be multiplied to you.[4]

Two observations will give us a sense of the significance of this letter opening for the letter as a whole. First, they are "chosen, strangers in the world"—that is, they are God's elect *and* they are alienated from their own worlds. In other words, their lives are a paradox: honored by God and chosen by God, but dishonored and forced to the margins of social life in their own villages and towns. This is an important observation because we tend to think that if all is right between God and God's people, then should God's people not flourish in their own hometowns and in the world at large? We do not easily correlate rejection within the human family with honorable status before God. Peter writes this letter to address just this sort of problem. Drawing on the experience of Israel in the Old Testament Peter develops the concept of "stranger" in what might be surprising ways, then. He associates being strangers in the world with God's election, and so with such scriptural themes as call and vocation, covenant, and journey. His perspective anticipates the words of the second-century *Epistle to Diognetus*, which develop this idea more fully:

> For Christians are no different from other people in terms of their country, language or customs. Nowhere do they inhabit cities of their own, use a strange dialect, or live life out of the ordinary. . . . They live in their respective countries, but only as resident aliens; they participate in all things as citizens, and they endure all things as foreigners. Every foreign territory is a homeland for them, every homeland foreign territory. They marry like everyone else and have children, but they do not expose them once they are born. They share their meals but not their sexual partners. They are found in the flesh but do not live according to the flesh. They live on earth but participate in the life of heaven. They are obedient to the laws that have been made, and by their own lives they supersede the laws. They love everyone and are persecuted by all. They are not understood and they are condemned. They are put to death and made alive. They are impoverished and make many rich. They lack all things and abound in everything. They are dishonored and they are exalted in their dishonors. (5:1-14)[5]

The first observation, then, concerns the plight of Christians: God's chosen ones, scorned by the world at large. Second, Peter uses three parallel phrases to underscore that being rejected by human beings does not entail having been rejected by God. His audience may be strangers in the world, treated like aliens who do not really belong here, but they have been chosen:

- according to the foreknowledge of God the Father,
- in the sanctification of the Spirit,
- because of the obedience and sprinkling of the blood of Jesus Christ.

Peter thus documents, first, that life on the margins of the world is not a denial of one's chosen status before God. More important, though, he shows that it is precisely because of the work of the Father, Son, and Holy Spirit in the lives of believers that they are being rejected. How could it be otherwise? Did the world not reject Jesus? Should we not anticipate, then, that the world would reject those who have been chosen by God and made holy by God's Spirit?

I have gone into some detail here in order to show how the phrase "according to the foreknowledge of God the Father" functions within 1 Peter. Divine choice and alien status are deeply rooted in God's purpose as this comes to expression in the Scriptures, so the dissonance of present life, chosen by God but held in contempt in society, is neither a surprise to God nor a contradiction of his plan.

Removed from the work this phrase performs in the presentation of Christian life in 1 Peter, though, this reference to God's foreknowledge came to support what Wesley regarded as a problematic, even unbiblical idea of predestination. As a result, in his *Explanatory Notes upon the New Testament,* he departs from his more usual routine of providing a word of historical background here, an explanation of an important term there. Instead, he outlines a full-blown theological essay on foreknowledge and predestination.

What is predestination? It is not easy to give a straightforward answer, since there are varieties of views in the Christian tradition. Wesley's definitions derive from Calvin's writings and from formalized confessions of faith penned in the sixteenth and seventeenth centuries:

> "Out of the general corruption," says the French Church, "he [God] draws those whom he has elected; leaving the others in the same corruption, according to his immovable decree." "By the decree of God," says the Assembly of English and Scotch Divines, "some are predestinated unto everlasting life, others foreordained to everlasting death." "God has once for all," says Mr. Calvin, "appointed, by an eternal and unchangeable decree, to whom he would give salvation, and whom he would devote to destruction." (*Inst.,* cap. 3, sec. 7)[6]

In other words, for Wesley, predestination could be understood thus: "By virtue of an eternal, unchangeable, irresistible decree of God, one part of humankind are infallibly saved, and the rest infallibly damned; it being impossible that any of the former should be damned, or that any of the latter should be saved."[7] This is the view that Wesley encountered—and countered. In fact, predestination was a key theological battleground in Wesley's day, and his engagement in the discussion was motivated in no small part by the influence of Calvinism within the Methodist movement. In his sermon on Romans 8:32, "Free Grace," for example, Wesley outlined seven arguments against this notion of predestination:

1. Predestination makes preaching unnecessary and thus nullifies one of the ordinances of God.
2. Predestination undermines holiness. After all, "if a sick man knows that he must unavoidably die or unavoidably recover, though he knows not which, it is not reasonable for him to take any medication at all" (§11).
3. Predestination obstructs the work of the Holy Spirit to bring assurance to the believer and so leads to despair.
4. Predestination destroys the zeal of believers toward works of mercy, such as feeding the hungry or clothing the naked.
5. Predestination renders needless the whole Christian revelation.
6. Predestination introduces contradictions into the message of the Bible.
7. Predestination is an insult to God, since it denies God's justice and mercy and portrays God as having done the work of the devil in leading people to the gates of hell.

In the place of this problematic notion of predestination, Wesley substitutes his teaching on free grace. This is that God gives his grace to everyone, even if not everyone chooses to receive this gift. To everyone the choice is put, to choose life, to repent, to come and taste.

What, then, of Wesley's reading of 1 Peter 1:1-2: "chosen...according to the foreknowledge of God the Father"? The context within which Wesley reads this text is the theological controversy in which he is enmeshed in eighteenth-century England, and this moves him to a discussion that may stretch us philosophically and theologically.

Wesley's opening salvo is his denial that God has the kind of foreknowledge that we humans might attribute to God. With the language of "foreknowledge," Wesley writes, God has adopted human vocabulary that is capable of speaking only partially of God's reality. Peter, then, is simply using language that would be understandable to people, rather than describing what is more accurately true of God.

> Strictly speaking, there is no foreknowledge, no more than after-knowledge, with God: but all things are known to him as present from eternity to eternity. This is therefore nothing more than an instance of the divine condescension to our lower capacities.[8]

Put simply, what is at stake here is how we view time, and particularly how we understand God's relation to time.

Wesley held a view that is different from what many of us assume about time, though his view was consistent with that of a number of early church fathers, and of an important figure in philosophical and theological discussions about time and eternity, Boethius (*ca.* A.D. 480–*ca.* 525). We think of time in linear terms—say, from the past to the present to the future. Boethius thought that eternity both included and transcended time. Since God inhabits eternity, it follows that all of time is present to God at once. It makes no sense to say that God "foreknew" such-and-such an event because God knows all things. We might experience time in terms of the past, present, and future, but this is not God's experience. This is because nothing is earlier or later than eternity, which God inhabits. Wesley himself knew and embraced the work of Boethius, and this is the basis of his claim that it is absurd to use the term "foreknowledge" with reference to God. Wesley goes on to urge that God's knowledge of all things does not cause things to happen.

Because these two related points may be hard to grasp, we ought to hear Wesley's words at length. First, let us review Wesley's understanding of time:

> [W]hen we speak of God's *foreknowledge* we do not speak according to the nature of things, but after the manner of humans. For if we speak properly there is no such thing as either

foreknowledge or *after-knowledge* in God. All time, or rather all eternity (for time is only that small fragment of eternity allotted to human beings) being present to him at once, he does not know one thing before another, or one thing after another, but sees all things in one point of view, from everlasting to everlasting. As all time, with everything that exists therein, is present with him at once, so he sees at once whatever was, is, or will be to the end of time.

God's experience of time is not the same as our own. Instead, for Wesley, God is omniscient in that God knows all things past, present, and future, because what happened in the past, what is happening in the present, and what will happen in the future—all understood according to the way we mark time—are always present to God. But if God knows all things, does this not mean that God causes all things? Not at all!

But observe: we must not think they are because he knows them. No; he knows them because they are. Just as I (if one may be allowed to compare the things of humans with the deep things of God) now know the sun shines. Yet the sun does not shine because I know it: but I know it because it shines. My knowledge takes it as true that the sun shines, but does not in any way cause it. In like manner God knows that humanity sins; for he knows all things. Yet we do not sin because he knows it: but he knows it because we sin. And his knowledge takes it as true that we sin, but does not in any way cause it. In a word, God looking on all ages from the creation to the consummation as a moment, and seeing at once whatever is in the hearts of all the people, knows everyone that does or does not believe in every age or nation. Yet what he knows, whether faith or unbelief, is in no way caused by his knowledge. People are as free in believing, or not believing, as if he did not know it at all.[9]

Wesley's view of time is thus key to his understanding of foreknowledge and predestination.

It remains, then, to inquire into the true meaning of predestination. For Wesley, God's "fore-appointment" consists in this: (1) whoever believes will be saved from the guilt and power of sin; (2) whoever endures until the end shall be saved eternally;

and (3) whoever receives the gift of faith thereby becomes the child of God, and receives the gift of the Holy Spirit so that they are enabled to live as Christ lived.

The way Wesley lays out the life of faith is sometimes called "synergistic," meaning that the life of faith requires cooperation between God and the person of faith. As Wesley himself puts it, predestination involves both God and the human being; at every step along the way "[God's] promise and [human] duty go hand in hand. All is a free gift; and yet such is the gift, that the final result depends on our future obedience."[10]

We are a long way from the opening words of 1 Peter, we may think. We might even wonder if Peter himself would be amazed at what has become of what might have seemed so simple a phrase, "chosen . . . according to the foreknowledge of God the Father"! Or we might wonder how Peter would respond to Wesley's claim, "God looking on all ages from the creation to the consummation as a moment, and seeing at once whatever is in the hearts of all the people, knows everyone that does or does not believe in every age or nation." In reality, though, what is crucial to Wesley in this whole discussion is not at all alien to Peter's message. Wesley takes a circuitous route to get there, but this is because of the terrain of the theological skirmishes he was forced to navigate in eighteenth-century Britain. But the synergism for which Wesley argued is no more important to Wesley than it was to Peter.

We may recall that Peter's audience consists of followers of Christ who live paradoxical lives. They are chosen of God but strangers in the world. As strangers in the world, they are the brunt of the world's scorn, insults, and shame. How will they respond? Peter instructs them along two paths at once. On the one hand, he affirms in no uncertain terms their having been chosen by God, their having been made holy by the Holy Spirit, their having been liberated by the atoning death of Jesus. In the world, they are dishonored, but before God they are honorable indeed. On the other hand, he calls them to certain behaviors in the world. They are to follow the example of Christ:

> For to this you have been called, because Christ also suffered for you, leaving you an example, so that you should follow in his steps.

"He committed no sin,
and no deceit was found in his mouth."
When he was abused, he did not return abuse; when he suffered, he did not threaten; but he entrusted himself to the one
who judges justly. (1 Pet 2:21-23)

They are to set aside the immorality of their former lives. They
are to forgo retaliation for the abuse they suffer. And they are to
take up such Christian practices as doing good, practicing hospitality, and extending themselves in acts of mutual love and service to one another. This is the promise they have: "And after you
have suffered for a little while, the God of all grace, who has
called you to his eternal glory in Christ, will himself restore, support, strengthen, and establish you" (1 Pet 5:10).

Questions for Reflection and Discussion

1. James and 1 Peter are concerned with exiles and Christians living at the margins of society. Are you or have you ever met someone who is an exile or new to this country? What might it be like
to live in exile?
2. For some, trials can produce endurance that guides them toward maturity. For others, trials lead only to failure, bitterness,
and a sense of hopelessness. How have your trials made you a
better person? What distinguishes the person who gains from trials and the person who is overwhelmed by trials? How can we
encourage persons to profit from their trials?
3. How is friendship with Jesus different from friendship with the
world?
4. Have you ever been rejected or suffered because of your faith?
Have you ever been in a situation where your faith was a problem
to the people you were with? What happened?
5. The doctrine or idea of predestination is difficult and confusing
for many. How do you understand it? How can Wesley help us
better understand and explain what it means?
6. Why is it important to lead a moral life? What difference does
it make to your relationship with God? What do you consider to
be immoral behavior?
7. Christ calls us to do good, practice hospitality, and extend our-

selves in acts of mutual love and service. If you had to give a grade, how would you evaluate your church's behavior when it comes to doing good, practicing hospitality, and extending itself in acts of love and service? Who is easy for your church to reach? Who does your church have trouble reaching? Why? Is your church's ministry primarily focused on itself or people outside the church?

8. In the Communion ritual in *The United Methodist Hymnal,* Christians are called to "joyful obedience." What does it mean to be obedient to Christ?

10

1 John

Whenever John Wesley wrote of 1 John, he often did so with near-unprecedented exuberance and appreciation. For example, after discussing a matter arising from John's first letter, he wrote: "It is highly probable there never were any children of God, from the beginning of the world unto this day, who were farther advanced in the grace of God and the knowledge of our Lord Jesus Christ than the apostle John at the time when he wrote these words."[1]

On more than one occasion, he upheld the style and content of 1 John as an example for all preachers. In a journal entry of 18 July 1765, he noted,

> In the evening I began expounding the deepest part of the holy Scripture, namely, the first Epistle of St. John, by which, above all other, even inspired writings, I advise every young preacher to form his or her style. Here are sublimity and simplicity together, the strongest sense and the plainest language! How can any one that would "speak as the oracles of God" use harder words than are found here?

Similarly, hear his journal notation of 5 January 1787: "I love St. John's style as well as matter." Wesley picks up this same motif in his preface to volumes 5–8 of "Sermons on Several Occasions." Advising preachers, he writes: " 'All who speak' in the name of God 'should speak as the oracles of God.' And if they would imitate any part of these above the rest, let it be the first Epistle of St. John. This is the style, the most excellent style, for every gospel preacher. And let them aim at no more ornament than they find in that sentence which is the sum of the whole gospel: 'We love him because he hath first loved us' " (§6).

It is easy to get the impression that, were Wesley stranded on a deserted island with only one book of the Bible, he would prefer that it be 1 John. "How plain, how full, and how deep a compendium of genuine Christianity!" he wrote on 1 September 1763. And again on 9 November 1772: "I began to expound . . . that compendium of all the Holy Scriptures, the First Epistle of St. John." Of course, Wesley uses the term "compendium" of other texts, too—most notably, the Sermon on the Mount (Matt 5–7) and Paul's famous "chapter on love," 1 Corinthians 13, both of which were for him compendia of "true religion."

Among NT letters, 1 John is relatively short, about 2,150 words in the Greek text. That Wesley refers to it almost 440 times in his sermons is thus all the more remarkable.[2] We have five sermons from Wesley on 1 John:

- Sermon 19: "The Great Privilege of Those That Are Born of God" (1 John 3:9)
- Sermon 55: "On the Trinity" (1 John 5:7)
- Sermon 62: "The End of Christ's Coming" (1 John 3:8)
- Sermon 77: "Spiritual Worship" (1 John 5:20)
- Sermon 78: "Spiritual Idolatry" (1 John 5:21)

Why 1 John?

Why was Wesley attracted to 1 John? Although he never answers this question directly, it is not hard to see why he would have turned so often to this New Testament letter. So many of Wesley's defining theological interests are here that it is hard to say whether Wesley turned to 1 John because Wesley's theological concerns were so well-developed in these few pages or because Wesley held these theological concerns due to his having been so fully formed by this letter. As with most chicken-and-egg questions, it is hard to know which came first and, in all probability, the answer is a little of both.

First John is cataloged with the New Testament collection of general or catholic letters—that is, letters whose audience is not narrowly specified. Wesley noticed the lack of a specified audience and concluded that 1 John was written "not to any particular church, but to all the Christians of that age; and in them to the whole Christian church in all succeeding ages." It lacks all the usual markers of a letter. It has no salutation and no addressee, for example. In fact, it has more the look of a written sermon than that of a letter. Wesley calls it a "tract," and summarizes its aim as confirming to all Christians everywhere "the happy and holy communion of the faithful with God and Christ, by describing the marks of that blessed state."[3]

Contemporary students of the three Johannine letters note how these letters, when read together, suggest a network of related churches struggling with false teaching and false prophets (for example, 1 John 2:18-22, 26; 4:1-6; 2 John 7). The author, whom we will call John, is actually named "the elder" in 2 John 1 and 3 John 1; he writes to encourage his readers to continue embracing and putting into play in their lives the truth that they had received—and, in doing so, to ward off the influence of false teachers.

Three aspects of John's message are especially interesting when read within the context of Wesley's interests:

(1) Assurance. John himself provides a general rationale for having written this letter: "I write these things to you who believe in the name of the Son of God, so that you may know that you have eternal life" (5:13). Among competing voices about the nature of genuine faith and authentic faithfulness, how can one be sure? Who are the genuine followers of Christ? John sets out three criteria:

- Obedience—"Now by this we may be sure that we know him, if we obey his commandments" (2:3; see 2:3-6, 17, 29; 3:4-10).
- Love for one another—"If we love one another, God lives in us, and his love is perfected in us" (4:12; see 3:10, 16-20; 4:21).
- Witness of the Spirit—"By this we know that he abides in us, by the Spirit that he has given us" (3:24; see 3:24–4:3; 4:13-16a).

For Wesley, it was vital that one's Christian experience align itself with and thus confirm Christian doctrine. So he taught that Christians might experience assurance that they were God's children. This experience must not be reduced to frothy emotionalism but was a divine conviction at work in a person's inner being. Wesley's insight on 1 John 3:24 is worth repeating: The Spirit that God has given us "witnesses with our spirits that we are his children, and brings forth his fruits of peace, love, holiness."[4] To put this somewhat differently, the witness of the Spirit, for 1 John, is realized in the Spirit's work to generate in the lives of believers the other two marks of assurance: obedience and mutual love.

(2) Theology and Ethics. Taking the short step from the end of the third chapter of 1 John into the fourth, we see another aspect of the Spirit's work: "By this you know the Spirit of God: every spirit that confesses that Jesus Christ has come in the flesh is from God, and every spirit that does not confess Jesus is not from God" (4:2-3).

Apparently, the false prophets against whom John wrote denied the incarnation (see 2:22, 25; 5:1, 6; 2 John 7). In denying that Jesus, God's Son, was really a human being, they misconstrued what it means to confess Jesus as Christ. Wesley observes that the coming of Christ "presupposes, contains, and draws after it the whole doctrine of Christ,"[5] and so recognizes the christological pivot-point of this text. What we must also take seriously, though, is what follows theologically from the doctrine of the incarnation. To say that God became flesh (see John 1:14) is to make magnificent statements both about God and about life in this world. In the incarnation, God affirmed the profound significance of human life. To deny the incarnation, then, is to undermine the church's understanding of God and of God's Son and also to reject the significance of human life in this world.

We can see where this way of thinking would take us. If life in this world lacks importance, then why worry with sin? with holiness? with love for one another? And so on. Theology and ethics are inseparable.

(3) Sin among Believers. From no less pedestrian a measure than word statistics, it is clear that "sin" is a major preoccupation of 1 John. The Greek verb *hamartanō*, "to sin," is concentrated in

1 John more than in any other New Testament book, and the noun, *hamartia* ("sin"), occurs in a higher concentration only in Romans. First John also has the highest concentration of the Greek term *skotia*, usually translated "darkness" and signifying not only lack of insight into matters of faith but also fellowship with evil or the rule of evil itself. Yet, as Wesley himself is quick to point out, 1 John is addressed to believers, albeit to followers of Christ at various stages of Christian growth. What are we to make of believers who sin? This was a major preoccupation with Wesley, motivated by his teaching on holiness.

"Those Who Have Been Born of God Do Not Sin" (1 John 3:9)

Central to Wesley's discussion in what follows is the following passage in 1 John 3:

> Everyone who commits sin is guilty of lawlessness; sin is lawlessness. You know that he was revealed to take away sins, and in him there is no sin. No one who abides in him sins; no one who sins has either seen him or known him. Little children, let no one deceive you. Everyone who does what is right is righteous, just as he is righteous. Everyone who commits sin is a child of the devil; for the devil has been sinning from the beginning. The Son of God was revealed for this purpose, to destroy the works of the devil. Those who have been born of God do not sin, because God's seed abides in them; they cannot sin, because they have been born of God. (3:4-9)

How does Wesley navigate the nature of the Christian life in relation to a New Testament text like this one?

In his sermon "The Great Privilege of Those That Are Born of God," grounded in 1 John 3:9, Wesley covers again some of the ground he had tilled in an earlier sermon, "The Marks of the New Birth" (see chap. 4, above). Here, though, he moves on more fully to discuss the issue of sin in the believer. He sets as his aim, first, "to consider what is the proper meaning of that expression, 'whosoever is born of God'; and, second, to inquire in what sense those born of God 'do not commit sin' " (§4). These reflections open up a third problem, however: "Does sin precede or follow the loss of faith?" (§III.1).

First, then, who is born of God? Wesley begins with his well-developed distinction between justification and new birth:

> Justification and the new birth are in point of time inseparable from each other, yet are they easily distinguished as being not the same, but things of a widely different nature. Justification implies only a relative, the new birth a real, change. God in justifying us does something *for* us: in begetting us again he does the work *in* us. The former changes our outward relation to God, so that of enemies we become children; by the latter our inmost souls are changed, so that of sinners we become saints. The one restores us to the favor, the other to the image of God. The one is the taking away the guilt, the other the taking away the power, of sin. So that although they are joined together in point of time, yet are they of wholly distinct natures. (§2)

Accordingly, he is able to segregate for further exploration the experience of new birth, particularly for the purpose of emphasizing the experience of real change in the life of the believer. This is "a vast inward change; a change wrought in the soul by the operation of the Holy Spirit, a change in the whole manner of our existence; for from the moment we are 'born of God' we live in quite another manner than we did before; we are, as it were, in another world" (§I.1).

This image of "another world" ought to be taken with utmost seriousness, so radical is the change of new birth. Prior to their being born anew, people are surrounded by this other world, the world involving spiritual matters, but they feel nothing of it, nor do they see or hear anything, since their senses are still closed up. They live in darkness. But as the newborn infant experiences the wonderful transition from the womb to the outside world, so the newly born believer experiences the world in an altogether new way.

> But when they are born of God, born of the Spirit, how is the manner of their existence changed! ... The Spirit or breath of God is immediately inspired, breathed into the new-born soul; and the same breath which comes from, returns to God. As it is

continually received by faith, so it is continually rendered back by love, by prayer, and praise, and thanksgiving—love and praise and prayer being the breath of every soul truly born of God. And by this new kind of spiritual respiration, spiritual life is not only sustained but increased day by day. (§I.8)

Their eyes have been opened, so that they see the mercy and promises of God. Their ears are opened, so that they hear and obey the voice of God. They now know the peace of God, joy in the Holy Spirit, and the love of God that penetrates the hearts of those who believe in Christ Jesus.

It is here that we reach a transition in Wesley's sermon. The new birth is like the continuous process of respiration—breathing in the love of God and life from God, breathing in the gracious influence of the Holy Spirit, breathing out unceasing love, and praise, and prayer. Here is the point of transition. If justification removes the guilt of sin and the new birth takes away the power of sin, then, following the language of 1 John 3, it can be said of the reborn that they "do not sin." As long as "God's seed abides in them; they cannot sin" (§II.1).

How to make sense of John's statements about sin has troubled readers for centuries. Who does not sin? Who, really, "cannot" sin? Christian experience might lead us to the conclusion that John refers only to Christ, since Christ alone was without sin—but this hardly seems to be the affirmation John wants to make. If it were not for John's language about present experience, perhaps we could imagine that John is speaking about the future, about life with God in heaven. Later in the letter, John refers to "sin that is mortal" (5:16). Although we might rightly think that no one in whom "God's seed abides" could commit such sin, there is nothing in 1 John 3 to suggest that this later "sin that leads to death" is in view earlier in the letter.

Another option would be to think that, by "sin," John refers to a certain category or level of "sin." This is the view developed by John Wesley:

By "sin" I here understand outward sin, according to the plain, common acceptation of the word: an actual, voluntary "transgression of the law"; of the revealed, written law of God; of any commandment of God acknowledged to be such at the time that it is transgressed. But "whoever is born of God," while they abide in faith and love and in the spirit of prayer and thanksgiving, not only "do not," but "cannot" thus "commit sin." So long as they thus believe in God through Christ and love him, and are pouring out their hearts before him, they cannot voluntarily transgress any command of God, either by speaking or acting what they know God has forbidden—so long as that "seed" that "remains in them" (that loving, praying, thankful faith) compels them to refrain from whatever they know to be an abomination in the sight of God. (§II.2)

Even with this important caveat, Wesley knows his view has problems. Such godly people as David in the Old Testament and Peter in the New, persons who are obviously born of God and persons of faith, participate in plain, undeniable sin. Wesley asks, "But how can this be reconciled with the assertion of St. John, if taken in the obvious literal meaning, that 'whoever is born of God does not commit sin'?" He continues,

I answer, what has been long observed is this: so long as "they that are born of God keep themselves" (which they are able to do, by the grace of God) "the wicked one does not touch them." But if they do not keep themselves, if they do not abide in the faith, they may commit sin even as other people. (§§II.6–7)

In effect, Wesley has just introduced the notion of "backsliding"—that is, the possibility of those who have been born of God experiencing a lapse in their faith. This is consistent with his view that the Christian life is a journey; even Christian perfection is not so much a destination to reach but a way of moving further along the path. If believers backslide, this is not because they lacked the spiritual resources to continue breathing in the love of God and life from God, breathing in the gracious influence of the Holy Spirit, then breathing out unceasing love, and praise, and prayer. It is, rather, because they failed to appropriate the grace of God given them. They did not respond to God's goodness by (in the words of 1 John) walking just as Jesus walked and loving as they had first been loved (2:6; 4:19).

It is easy therefore to understand how children of God might be moved from their own steadfastness, and yet the great truth of God, declared by the apostle, remains steadfast and unshaken. They did not keep themselves by that grace of God that was sufficient for him. They fell step by step, first into negative, inward sin—not "stirring up the gift of God" that was in them, not "watching in prayer," not "pressing on to the mark of the prize of the high calling"; then into positive, inward sin—inclining to wickedness in their hearts, giving way to some evil desire or temper. Next they lost their faith, their sight of a pardoning God, and consequently their love of God. And being then weak and like another people they were capable of committing even outward sin. (§II.7)

Wesley has just made a crucial move in his understanding of sin, focusing as he has on knowing, willful, voluntary acts of disobedience. He might be critiqued for this, since in contemporary neuroscience we are discovering more and more the degree to which how we behave is the product of largely unconscious processes in our brain. Anyone who has suffered even mild forms of addiction knows the problem—long-term thinking versus short-term desire. Neurobiologists, though, have begun to identify the neural correlates of the seven deadly sins, for example—sloth, lust, pride, anger, envy, greed, and gluttony—and to show how the brain's "reward system" is tied to these patterns of behavior quite apart from what we self-consciously think we want to be or do. Wesley's understanding of sin, with its focus on willful, voluntary behavior, thus seems to be problematic.

This criticism of Wesley may be wide of the mark, though. Wesley, of course, was not a neuroscientist, but it is interesting how his understanding of the human person—his psychology, so to speak—dovetails with contemporary brain research. This is suggested in this section of the sermon as he reflects on David (see 2 Sam 11):

He was "walking on the roof of his house," probably praising the God whom his soul loved, when he looked and saw Bathsheba. He felt a temptation, a thought which tended to evil. The Spirit of God did not fail to convince him of this. He doubtless heard and knew the warning voice. But he yielded in some measure to the thought, and the temptation began to prevail over him. Hereby his spirit was sullied. He saw God still; but it was more dimly than before. He loved God still; but not in the same degree, not with the same strength and ardor of affection. Yet God checked him again, though his spirit was grieved; and his voice, though fainter and fainter, still whispered, "Sin lies at the door" "look unto me, and be saved." But he would not hear. He looked again, not to God, but to the forbidden object, until nature was superior to grace, and kindled lust in his soul.

Wesley continues, "The eye of his mind was now closed again, and God vanished out of his sight. Faith, the divine, supernatural intercourse with God, and the love of God ceased together. He then rushed on as a horse into the battle, and knowingly committed the outward sin" (§II.8).

Although Wesley attaches the word *sin* only to this outward act, he understands that outward acts do not materialize out of thin air. They are the fruit of what Wesley called our "tempers" and "affections"—that is, the patterns of thinking, feeling, and believing that characterize our lives. These patterns shape and motivate certain patterns of behavior. For Wesley, then, much happens internally with David before, externally, he "rushed on as a horse into the battle, and knowingly committed the outward sin." As his sermon continues, he enumerates this process as "the unquestionable progress from grace to sin." Borrowing again the language of 1 John 3, he traces this progress, step-by-step:

> (1) The divine seed of loving, conquering faith remains in those who are "born of God." "They keep themselves," by the grace of God, and "cannot commit" sin. (2) A temptation arises, whether from the world, the flesh, or the devil, it matters not. (3) The Spirit of God gives them warning that sin is near, and bids them more abundantly watch in prayer. (4) They give way in some degree to the temptation, which now begins to grow pleasing to them. (5) The Holy Spirit is grieved; their faith is weakened, and their love of God grows cold. (6) The Spirit reproves them more sharply, saying, "This is the way; walk in it." (7) They turn away from the painful voice of God and listen to the pleasing voice of the tempter. (8) Evil desire begins and spreads in their soul, until faith and love vanish. (9) They are

then capable of committing outward sin, the power of the Lord having departed from them. (§II.9)

Reflecting on the progress from grace to nature in this way, Wesley concludes that inward sin leads to the initial loss of faith, and loss of faith to committing outward sin. The preventive of sin, then, is, of course, the grace of God, but also the faithful response to God's grace that grace itself calls forth and enables.

Returning to the metaphor of respiration, Wesley observes what is needed:

> the continual inspiration of God's Holy Spirit: God's breathing into the soul, and the soul's breathing back what it first receives from God; a continual action of God on the soul, and reaction of the soul on God; an unceasing presence of God, the loving, pardoning God, manifested to the heart, and perceived by faith; and an unceasing return of love, praise, and prayer, offering up all the thoughts of our hearts, all the words of our tongues, all the works of our hands, all our body, soul, and spirit, to be a holy sacrifice, acceptable unto God in Christ Jesus. (§III.2)

Put sharply, Wesley may *claim* that sin in 1 John 3 is limited to "an actual, voluntary 'transgression of the law,'" but his analysis of the problem takes us deeper into the human person. This demonstrates the necessity of transformation through grace not simply of outward behavior but especially of one's patterns of thinking, believing, feeling, *and* behaving.

Let us return to 1 John. In our text, 1 John 3:4-9, our author grounds the sinless Christian life above all in the work of Christ and, then, in the believer's commitment to living in the work of Christ. Note the following parallels:

Sin is lawlessness (v. 4).	Sin is of the devil (v. 8).
The Son of God came to take away sins (v. 5).	The Son of God came to destroy the work of the devil (v. 8).
No one who remains in Christ sins (v. 6).	Those who are born of God cannot sin (v. 9).

These parallels demonstrate, first, that the problem of sin has been addressed by Jesus Christ, the Son of God. Whatever else may be said, the claim that believers do not sin is grounded in the prior work of Christ, whose death on the cross addresses the problem of sin (see, for example, 1 John 1:7). Second, though, we find that sinlessness depends on a person's being born of God (v. 9) and on that person's remaining in Christ (v. 6). To help fill out John's meaning, observe the further parallel he sets out in verse 9:

> Those who have been born of God do not sin, because God's seed abides in them;
> [those who have been born of God] cannot sin, because they have been born of God.

This means that those who are born of God are those in whom the "seed," the good news of God's word (see Mark 4:3-20), has been planted *and* in whom this good news has taken root and flourished. The transformation brought about by the good news is not limited to a past event of implantation, for John has it that God's seed abides (it dwells, it takes up residence) in those born anew. At the same time that God's seed abides in those born of God, so also those who are born of God remain in Christ (v. 6). Insofar as this is the case, then sinning lies outside the lives of believers.

Against the background of 1 John, then, we may hear again in the foreground Wesley's respiratory image: continuously breathing in the influence of divine grace, continuously breathing out responses of faith, hope, and love. This is a good image not only for Wesley but also for 1 John.

Questions for Reflection and Discussion

1. Wesley makes a distinction between being a genuine or real Christian and simply being a Christian. How do you understand the difference?
2. Criteria for being a genuine Christian include obedience, love, and witness. By these, other people can see that we are living a Christian life. How important is it that others know that you are

a Christian? Can people tell you are a Christian by how you live your daily life?

3. God is at work in us, through us, with us, for us, and sometimes, in spite of us. Reflect on time when you saw God working through a person you know.

4. God calls us to obey his commandments and follow in the path that leads to life, and God also equips us and encourages us. How can you and your church equip and encourage people to follow the ways of God? How can we discern that we are really following the ways of God or if we are just doing what we think is best? Is there a difference? How does the Holy Spirit empower us to be obedient followers? Is obedience a burdensome duty or a joyful gift for you?

5. In the hospital, patients sometimes receive breathing treatments so that they can develop their lungs to breathe more effectively. Wesley talks about breathing in the love of God, so that when we breathe out, we breathe out with acts of loving-kindness. How can we develop our spiritual "lungs" so that we can live a life of love more effectively?

6. Everyone has lapses such as lapses of memory and lapses of good judgment. Wesley suggests we also can have lapses of faith. During those times we backslide in our faith away from God. Have you ever backslid from your faith? What were those times like? What or who brought you back? What can bring others back? How does your witness affect how others see God at work in the world?

7. As new creatures in Christ, our eyes become open to a new world, according to Wesley. How do you see God at work in your life, in your church, in your community?

8. Loving God means walking in the light as he is in the light. How can we bring others into the light of Christ?

11

Revelation

> Preaching in the evening at Spitalfields on "Prepare to meet thy
> God," I largely showed the utter absurdity of the supposition
> that the world was to end that night. But notwithstanding all I
> could say, many were afraid to go to bed, and some wandered
> about in the fields, being persuaded that, if the world did not
> end, at least London would be swallowed up by an earthquake.
> I went to bed at my usual time, and was fast asleep by ten
> o'clock.

In this journal entry of 28 February 1763, Wesley demonstrated
that he was not one of those who were interested in predicting
the date of the end times. Previously, on 7 January of the same
year, he met with George Bell, hoping "to convince him of his mistakes, particularly that which he had lately adopted, that the end
of the world was to be on February 28th," but he was unsuccess-
ful. And this explains the apparent drama of 28 February.

To say that Wesley was unflappable in the face of a prophecy
dating the end of the world is not to say that he was unconcerned
with eschatology—that is, a Christian understanding of the end
times (combining two Greek words: *eschatos*, "end," + *logos*, "understanding of"). In fact, Wesley was far more at home with talk-
ing about the end times than he was with reading the book of
Revelation. As a result, we have only one sermon from Wesley on
the last book of the Bible:

• Sermon 64: "The New Creation" (Rev 21:5)

Wesley and the End Times

Wesley's eschatological interests were not speculative. We find in his written materials nothing like the maps of the prophetic future or mathematical calculations for dating the return of Christ that dot the landscape of the history of reading texts like Mark 13 or the book of Revelation. One way to get a handle on the sort of interest Wesley did have is with the concept of "backshadowing." Most of us are familiar with the concept of "foreshadowing" in literature. In foreshadowing, we find hints of what is to come, so that earlier parts of the story anticipate later parts. In "backshadowing," we have glimpses of the future that cast their shadows back on the present. These give us a sense of God's aims for the future and, in this way, show us what is of real consequence in the present. For Wesley, this backshadowing would do more than point the way. Visions of the future lay a claim on our lives, to be sure, but Wesley held that the life of the future was already breaking into the present. In this sense, the end points the way forward and draws us forward. We might imagine that eternal life was a future prospect of life together with God forever, for example. For Wesley, though,

> eternal life commences when it pleases the Father to reveal his Son in our hearts; when we first know Christ, being enabled to "call him Lord by the Holy Spirit"; when we can testify, our conscience bearing us witness in the Holy Ghost, "the life which I now live, I live by faith in the Son of God, who loved me, and gave himself for me." And then it is that happiness begins—happiness real, solid, substantial. Then it is that heaven is opened in the soul, that the proper, heavenly state commences, while the love of God, as loving us, is shed abroad in the heart, instantly producing love to all humankind: general, pure benevolence, together with its genuine fruits, lowliness, meekness, patience, contentedness in every state; an entire, clear, full acquiescence in the whole will of God, enabling us to "rejoice evermore, and in everything to give thanks." ("Spiritual Worship" §II.5)

This perspective coheres well with Jesus' teaching on the kingdom of God in the Gospels. Although anticipating the future realization of God's dominion over all, Jesus' message also underscores ways in which God's reign is a present reality. Similarly, we can anticipate the time when, in the words of Revelation 11:15, "the kingdom of the world has become the kingdom of our Lord and of his Messiah, and he will reign forever and ever." But Jesus can also make the cornerstone of his mission these words concerned with the present: "Now is the time! Here comes the kingdom of God!"—a message that has as its immediate corollary the call to "change your hearts and lives and trust the good news!" (Mark 1:15, my translation). Wesley articulated this kind of perspective in his notes on Matthew 3:2. Speaking of the kingdom of heaven, or the kingdom of God, he writes that this phrase refers not merely to "a future happy state in heaven, but a state to be enjoyed on earth; the proper disposition for the glory of heaven, rather than the possession of it."[1]

This idea of "backshadowing" is useful in another way. Wesley devotes a sermon to "the never-dying worm and the unquenchable fire," going into some detail regarding the nature and extent of damnation ("Of Hell"). To what end? Biblical teaching on hell, he states, serves as a constraint on the ungodly and as a means to discourage believers from drifting into sin.

> Are you tempted by pain either of body or mind? O compare present things with future. What is the pain of body that you do or may endure, to that of lying in a lake of fire burning with brimstone? What is any pain of mind, any fear, anguish, sorrow, compared to "the worm that never dies"? That never dies! This is the sting of all! As for our pains on earth, blessed be God, they are not eternal. . . . Suffer any pain, then, rather than come into that place of torment. (§III.3)

Similarly, in his sermon "The Great Assize," Wesley preaches on the scene of the final judgment. The unusual setting for this sermon, not a preaching hall or even a street corner but a court of law, presses Wesley to develop the ramifications of the last judgment in a peculiar way. He traces the eschatological events leading to the final judgment, then explains the basis of that judgment before turning to draw out the consequences of this vision of the end-time judgment. On the one hand, he speaks to earthly judges, reminding them that they engage provisionally in the work that God himself will perform finally. Accordingly, their judgments should take their measure from God's, and they should carry out their work knowing that they will be held accountable for it. More generally, all are called to live today in the shadow of that day, when one's eternal future is determined in light of the judgments made in this life. A sermon on the final judgment thus concludes with an evangelistic call:

> He stands in the midst! Sinner, does he not now, even now, knock at the door of your heart? O that you may know, at least "in this thy day," the things that belong to your peace! O that ye may now give yourselves to him who "gave himself for you," in humble faith, in holy, active, patient love! So will you rejoice with exceeding joy in his day, when he comes in the clouds of heaven. (§IV.5)

Wesley and the Book of Revelation

Consider the words with which Wesley begins his comments on the book of Revelation:

> It is scarcely possible for any that either love or fear God not to feel their hearts extremely affected in seriously reading either the beginning or the latter part of the Revelation. These, it is evidence, we cannot consider too much; but the intermediate parts I did not study at all for many years, as utterly despairing of understanding them, after the fruitless attempts of so many wise and good people.

Indeed, he goes on to admit, he might not have written on these "intermediate parts" at all had he not come across the work of Bengel, from whose work he borrows heavily in his own notes. Even so, Wesley acknowledges that he does not pretend to understand or explain all we find in Revelation, "this mysterious book."[2]

Undoubtedly, on any number of points, Wesley's dependence on Johann Albrecht Bengel in his *Explanatory Notes upon the New Testament* served him (and us) well. When it comes to this final book of the New Testament, however, we might have preferred that Wesley had taken us no further than his own interests in Revelation 1–3 and Revelation 21–22 ("the beginning and latter part of the Revelation") and left the remainder of Revelation 4–20 ("the intermediate part") in the realm of mystery. Instead, we find some of the most extensive commentary in all of the *Explanatory Notes,* including much that reflects far more the situation and judgments of the German theologian Johann Albrecht Bengel (1687–1752) than those of John, the visionary and prophet who wrote the book of Revelation (see Rev 1:9). One notorious example is Bengel's work on Revelation 13—thirteen pages of study notes with long lists of papal appointments, papal movements, propositions, and observations, all determined to excoriate the Catholic Church by identifying the papacy with the beast. "O reader, this is . . . a solemn warning from God! The danger is near. Be armed both against force and fraud, even with the whole armor of God. . . . The beast is the Papacy of the Roman Church, as it came to a point six hundred years since, stands now, and will for some time longer."[3]

Of all of the gains of biblical scholarship in the past two hundred years, perhaps none is as fortunate as the way it has taught us to raise questions about and pursue the significance of the book of Revelation. Because it is so alien in form and content to the rest of the Bible—and, indeed, to the rest of what generally passes for reading material—it has functioned for many less as Holy Scripture and more as a Rorschach test or an arsenal for end-time fantasies. Perhaps more widely, it has had no function at all, as people turned for spiritual nourishment and formation to the Pauline letters, for example, rather than to the Revelation of John.

In reality, there is a reason that Revelation seems strange to us. It is strange! That is, it comprises a form of writing with which we have little to compare. We can take solace from the fact that this book belongs to a family of similar writings dating roughly to the time it was written in the latter decade of the first century. And an important path into making sense of the book is to recognize that it draws much of its imagery and patterns of thought from the Old Testament prophets (like Ezekiel, Daniel, and Isaiah). In the end, though, Revelation is a mishmash piece of literature. In its opening verses, the book touches base with three ancient literary forms:

- *Revelation describes itself as an "apocalypse":* "The revelation of Jesus Christ" (1:1). The term "revelation" itself translates the Greek term *apokalypsis*—hence, "apocalypse" or "apocalyptic." Written within a narrative framework, it discloses a message from God mediated by an angel to John, portraying earthly life from a heavenly perspective in anticipation of end-time salvation. What is more, it is written within the context of the political, economic, and religious challenges of life as a minority people in the midst of a seemingly all-powerful empire. As such it is a narrative of resistance, demonstrating the character of faithful life over against the power structures and conventions of the wider world. Like other books of this kind, Revelation includes visions, fantastic images, an emphasis on the end time, a heightened understanding of God's authority and capacity to bring history to its proper conclusion, and a break between this world and the next.

- *Revelation identifies itself as a prophetic book:* "Blessed is the one who reads aloud the words of the prophecy" (1:3).[4] Although we tend to associate "prophecy" with "predicting the future," within the life of Israel and the early church, "prophecy" was less "foretelling" and more speaking on behalf of God as inspired by God's Spirit. This meant giving God's perspective on current events, resisting the perspectives and interpretations of reality offered by powers and authorities antagonistic to God's purposes, and challenging God's people to appropriate response in light of God's purpose.

- *Revelation presents itself as a pastoral letter:* "John to the seven churches that are in Asia: Grace to you and peace from him who is and who was and who is to come, and from the seven spirits who are before his throne, and from Jesus Christ, the faithful witness, the firstborn of the dead, and the ruler of the kings of the earth" (1:4-5; see 22:21 and chaps. 2–3). Like the New Testament letters, then, Revelation presents itself as correspondence written to provide consolation and encouragement, criticism and challenge, for its addressees. In this case, Revelation as a "letter" is addressed to certain churches in Asia Minor (see chaps. 2–3), and is thus a message concerned with concrete circumstances.

All of this reminds us that Revelation was written with first-century Christians in mind—not in order to be stored away for a future time when the events and characters it describes really began to happen and to walk the face of the earth. As Revelation 22:10 puts it, "Do not seal up the words of the prophecy of this book, for the time is near." To say it differently, Revelation envisions what was at the time of its writing *already* happening or *already* beginning to happen.

Does this mean that Revelation has no meaning for today? Of course not! The Gospel of Matthew and Paul's Letter to the Romans were written for first-century folks, too, but this does not mean that we are to relegate the message of these New Testament books to the mothballs of history. Among the several reasons that could be given for the continuing significance of Revelation is simply this: as Wesleyans, we read Revelation (as well as Philemon or 1 Corinthians or the Gospel of John) as Christian Scripture, as God's word to God's people. It is true, however, that for many of us, reading Revelation requires additional work as we seek to enter into the world it portrays and to hear and see what John heard and saw as divine word.

Reading Revelation as Wesleyans

Even the literary forms Revelation adopts remind us of how rooted in its own social and historical context the book is. However, through its images and symbols, Revelation ensures that its message is not time-bound to the church of the past. When John enters God's throne room in Revelation 4, he does not experience the worship only of a particular time in the late first century. Instead, he sees what really is, who God really is, what God's aims in history really are, and how God works in history to move all of creation toward the realization of his purpose. After all, this is the God "who is and who was and who is to come" (1:4), who accomplishes his redemptive plan through Jesus Christ, who can identify himself in these words: "I am the Alpha and the Omega, the first and the last, the beginning and the end" (22:13).

Revelation was written in a world ruled by the Roman Empire. From an earthly perspective, Rome might have seemed all-powerful, even irresistible in its military might, its political reach, and its economic extravagance. What seems so real to earthbound creatures is unmasked for what it is when seen from the heavens. Rome, the beast from the sea in John's vision in Revelation 13, has all the power of a Halloween costume; Rome is like a character in an evil masquerade party. Its power is not its own. Its power and authority are neither ultimate nor eternal. God, after all, is on the heavenly throne, and he will preside on earth as he already presides in heaven. This is good news, a word of encouragement, for all those oppressed by the mighty arm of earthly powers. But it is bad news, an alarming word of warning, for all who participate in or benefit from that same earthly power. From this heavenly perspective, then, John writes to unmask the powers and to call followers of Christ to bear witness to "real reality"—that is, through word and deed, and even through the giving up of their lives, to bear witness to the kingdom of God.

Strangely, the more we understand the message of Revelation in its first-century setting, the more we find ourselves at home in its pages and the more we grasp its message for all times, including our own. If Rome is the sea-beast of Revelation 13, this does not remove the stunning portrait of evil from our view as twenty-first-century readers. This is because Rome is for John only the latest power to masquerade as evil's puppet king. Rome is only the latest authority to claim for itself that ultimate allegiance of people that can only be directed toward God. The late first-century Roman Empire did not own these claims to power and these structures of oppression; these have continued even in the wake of Rome's decline and fall. Nor are our Christian brothers and sisters of Asia Minor in the waning years of the first century the last to struggle under imperial demands and exploitative systems. The question, then, is not simply how we read Revelation today, but rather how Revelation reads us. Let me highlight six themes:

(1) Revelation changes the way we see and respond to the world. As

much as any book in the Bible, Revelation recognizes how the glasses we wear determine what we can see and understand about the world around us. As the narrator of C. S. Lewis's *Magician's Nephew* has it, "[W]hat you see and hear depends a good deal on where you are standing: it also depends on what sort of person you are."[5] Not surprisingly, Revelation addresses both where we stand and what sort of people we are. Remember that, within John's revelatory experience, he stands not in a church in Asia Minor nor in the Coliseum of Rome, nor even on the "island called Patmos" (1:9). He stands in the heavens. He sees things from God's perspective, so he sees things as they really are. What is more, through his narrative he invites us to accompany him, so that we, too, see things as they really are. To do so, though, we need not only to travel with him to the throne room of God but also to allow our patterns of thinking, feeling, and believing to be dismantled and reassembled through binding ourselves to Jesus Christ, the Lamb of God, who is worthy to receive honor, dominion, and power by means of his humiliating death (Rev 5).

(2) Revelation orients all of life around the worship of God. The throne room has as its focal point God, surrounded by the world's creatures united in praise. Revelation itself is riddled with hymns of praise to God and to the Lamb. At the end of the book, John is overcome (Who would not be?) by his visionary experience, so he falls down and worships the angel who has revealed to him these things. But the angel says, "You must not do that! I am a fellow servant with you and your comrades the prophets, and with those who keep the words of this book." And then the angel gives the directive that summarizes the whole book: "Worship God!" (22:8-9).

The opposite of true worship, idolatry, comes in various guises, but always it is a counter to the first command, "You shall have no other gods before me" (Exod 20:3). One can serve God or one can buy into the possibilities and paths offered by a distracting world, but one cannot do both at once. For readers of Revelation, worship is also the antidote to the sin of despair—that is, the sin of acting as though what we see and hear and experience in day-to-day life were all there is. Here are two problems: The first is life lived under the horrific illusion that *this* world is the object of our hope, that *this* is the destination for which the journey of faith was begun, and thus that *this* is our genuine home. The second is abandonment of hope in the face of wrongful suffering. The first forgets that we live in the shadow of Babylon, while the second assumes that Babylon has the last word. The first assumes that courageous resistance in the world is unnecessary, while the second assumes that courageous resistance in the world is useless. The effect is the same—capitulation to the world's ways of making sense of life. This is a failure to find one's true self and vocation in the worship of the one God, "the one who was seated on the throne," who said,

> "See, I am making all things new." Also he said, "Write this, for these words are trustworthy and true." Then he said to me, "It is done! I am the Alpha and the Omega, the beginning and the end. To the thirsty I will give water as a gift from the spring of the water of life. Those who conquer will inherit these things, and I will be their God and they will be my children." (21:5-7)

(3) Revelation resists alternative portraits of world events. Let me illustrate by calling upon the theologian James McClendon's idea of a "contest of stories." He observes that, growing up in the United States, from an early age, we learn a consensus story that we take as good and right. This story has elements like these: brave pilgrims set out in search of freedom from tyranny; they find the promised land where they must conquer the indigenous population as well as battle for independence; they engage in civil war in order to liberate all persons; they move westward across the continent, to realize their dreams, depending only on themselves; and, blessed by God, they are able to fight for the liberty of those outside their borders as well. McClendon did not want to belittle the American Story, which has underwritten hope for millions of families. Nevertheless, he could not help noticing one of its most constant elements: violence is necessary if people are to experience liberty. Contrast this, he says, with a story that pivots upon a savior who comes on a donkey, is acclaimed as the prince of peace, and in whose death peace is won.

The pressing question for McClendon is this: "Which story, the cultural or the biblical one, really engages me?"[6] McClendon's contest of stories is like a parable for making sense of Revelation.

Here is the power of the devil, on display through the devil's minions, Rome and Rome's religious and propaganda machines—irresistible and incontestable, an economic powerhouse, bringer of peace and tranquillity to all in its borders. Here is the Lamb, standing in the midst of the throne as if it had been slaughtered, declared worthy to receive power, wealth, wisdom, might, honor, glory, and blessing *because it was slaughtered by none other than the almighty hand of Rome itself.* Here are two competing stories. Both cannot be true. The story of the lamb seems uninviting, unlikely, *and yet this is the lamb whose sacrificial death spells the undoing of the power of evil.* The result, then, is not only a competing vision of present life but, just as important, the promise of a transformed future.

(4) Revelation challenges the church just as it critiques the world-at-large. Given what I have summarized so far, it might be easy to imagine that Revelation has positioned its prophetic armaments against the world. This is only partially true. Revelation engages in a sustained criticism of the structures and values and practices of a world that aligns itself against God. But Revelation, we must remind ourselves, was not written "to the world." It was written to the church, which so easily finds itself cozy in the world. Notice in the opening letters of chapters 2–3 the presence of the Nicolaitans in Ephesus (2:6) and Pergamum (2:12), and of followers of Jezebel at Pergamum (2:20) and of Balaam at Thyatira (2:18). With these references, John identifies the twin problems of idolatry and immorality—*inside* the church. This is nothing less than the result of the church's willingness to lose itself through assimilation into the world defined and orchestrated by Rome.

(5) Revelation especially challenges the church on issues of faith and wealth. Given his hyper-concerns with money, had Wesley found himself more at home in the pages of Revelation, he would undoubtedly have challenged his audiences with Revelation's thoroughgoing analysis of the idolatry of wealth. Here we find an unrelenting barrage of critical assessment. Behind John's Revelation is the reality of empire. Rome built and extended its empire to meet the demands of Rome's own population, to increase Rome's own wealth, and to enhance Rome's own honor. It built an amazing network of roads and opened up sea-lanes for the

primary purpose of feeding itself. The much-exalted *Pax Romana*, "Roman peace," was oriented toward this: developing and using the economy of the entire civilized world in the service of Rome. Within John's Revelation is a critique of the empire. Rome is a mistress harlot, a city whose luxurious lifestyle is maintained at its lovers' expense (see 17:1-6; 18:3, 9, 16). Rome's network of economic interests includes those who enjoy the celebrated benefits of *Pax Romana*—unity, security, and stability—and who gain from Rome's economic dominance—kings, merchants, mariners (see 18:9-19). Here is the problem: Rome's economic luxuriousness is built on the back of Rome's own subjects who participate in, even embrace, their own exploitation. Ironically, they even mourn when God's judgment falls on Rome (18:9, 11, 17). They are taken in by Rome's luxury. They are exploited but blind, bedazzled by Roman propaganda (see 14:8; 17:2; 18:3, 23). What is more, this wealth-centered existence has found its way into the church at Laodicea, which is then criticized for its reliance on wealth (3:14-22). Compare the words of the Spirit to the church at Smyrna, who is comforted in its lack (2:8-11). Finally, John envisions a time when the wealth of this world has been condemned, when faithful followers of Christ will experience true wealth, God's own bounty. Theirs will be a wedding celebration (19:7, 9, 17-18), the water of life will be available without cost (21:6), and heaven itself will have a glory and radiance beyond what even Rome at the height of its splendor could ever have imagined (21:11-21).

(6) Revelation's picture of costly discipleship involves risky, engaged resistance. By the time of John's writing of the book of Revelation, resistance to the ways of Rome already had a long pedigree. Included in the well-known and practiced options among the Jewish people was guerrilla-warfare-type action as well as organized military resistance, and withdrawal from society-at-large in order to nurture an ideal community life away from the world and its challenges to faithfulness. John's Revelation takes neither path. Nowhere within its pages are followers of Christ called to take up arms against the Roman political, economic, and religious powerhouse. Nowhere within its pages are followers of Christ urged to come away from the world into a Christian enclave or church-compound separate from the world. On the one hand,

John envisions that God's saving agenda is not limited to the hearts of Christ's followers. The kingdom of God is not limited to spiritual matters only, but embraces all of life, including the transformation of the political world. Leaving the world to its own devices is therefore not an option. On the other hand, John's readers are told repeatedly that they are to hold fast to the faith so that they participate in the conquering of evil. What, then, are the weapons of their warfare? John depicts a strange arsenal:

- "Be faithful until death, and I will give you the crown of life" (2:10).
- "But they have conquered him by the blood of the Lamb and by the word of their testimony, for they did not cling to life even in the face of death" (12:11).
- "Here is a call for the endurance of the saints, those who keep the commandments of God and hold fast to the faith of Jesus" (14:12).

Remember that John himself has been exiled "because of the word of God and the testimony of Jesus," and that he shares with his readers "the persecution and the kingdom and the patient endurance" (1:9). Putting texts like these together with what we have already seen, we find a short list of armaments for Christian participation in God's transformation of all things:

- worship of God
- bearing verbal, prophetic witness against the powers, even if doing so leads to the loss of one's own life through martyrdom
- navigating life according to the compass set by Jesus' own endurance and faithfulness in the face of opposition and death

To put it differently, the basic Christian response to which John calls his readers is nothing less (and nothing more) than ongoing, stubborn allegiance to the kingdom of God. This requires loyalty to the seemingly powerless politics of the kingdom rather than imitating the oppressive politics of the beast.

To some, John may appear to be counseling passivity. Nothing could be farther from the truth. It is, rather, a recognition that the cause of evil is advanced, not curtailed, when evil practices are taken up by those who seek to counter evil. Recall that John portrays the dragon—"that ancient serpent, who is called the Devil and Satan, the deceiver of the whole world" (12:9)—as exercising its power through Rome. Rome itself is not the evil power. Remembering this, it becomes obvious that the evil one would be more than ready to allow others, even well-meaning followers of Christ, to take up the mantle of the dragon. The dragon welcomes all partners. What appears to be John's passive response to the beast, then, is actually his invitation to a vocation of resistance on the side of the politics of the crucified Christ, against the politics of coercion and violence.

Wesley and the New Creation

Wesley's lone sermon from Revelation takes a single phrase from Revelation 21:5 as its text: "Behold, I make all things new" (ASV). However, his preaching ranges across the images of newness we find in the first paragraph of this chapter in Revelation:

> Then I saw a new heaven and a new earth; for the first heaven and the first earth had passed away, and the sea was no more. And I saw the holy city, the new Jerusalem, coming down out of heaven from God, prepared as a bride adorned for her husband. And I heard a loud voice from the throne saying, "See, the home of God is among mortals. He will dwell with them as their God; they will be his peoples, and God himself will be with them; he will wipe every tear from their eyes. Death will be no more; mourning and crying and pain will be no more, for the first things have passed away." And the one who was seated on the throne said, "See, I am making all things new." Also he said, "Write this, for these words are trustworthy and true." (21:1-5)

The picture John paints is stunning on its own merits, and worth contemplation. Wesley himself seems awestruck as he considers it:

> What a strange scene is here opened to our view! How remote from all our natural apprehensions! . . . It must be allowed that

after all the researches we can make, still our knowledge of the great truth delivered to us in these words is exceedingly short and imperfect. As this is a point of genuine revelation, beyond the reach of all our natural faculties, we cannot penetrate far into it, nor form any adequate conception of it. But it may be an encouragement to those who have in any degree tasted of the powers of the world to come to go as far as we can go, interpreting Scripture by Scripture, according to the analogy of faith. (§§1–2)

Wesley's opening is interesting not only for the wonder Revelation 21 has inspired in him but also for its straightforward claim about how to make sense of a text that challenges our abilities to interpret. He identifies two interpretive principles:

(1) *Interpreting Scripture with Scripture* was a Reformation principle drawn from the supposition that the Bible was written to be understood by God's people. Hence, when someone ran across a "hard text"—that is, a text that could not be easily deciphered—then one could appeal to the plain sense of those texts that were easily understood. Apparently, Wesley regarded Revelation 21 as just such a text: "we cannot penetrate far into it, nor form any adequate conception of it." As a result, he was willing to range across the Old and New Testaments to find what light might be shed on it.

(2) A number of Reformers likewise appealed to the *analogy of faith,* though this interpretive principle was actually at work much earlier, in the first centuries of the church. There we find the language of the "rule of faith" or the "rule of truth." Generally speaking, the analogy of faith refers to the doctrinal faith of the church. For example, in many congregations today the Apostles' Creed is recited weekly or monthly. This is a narrative account of the faith of the church structured around the Christian affirmation of the triune God. How does it guide biblical interpretation? It is not that we read the creed back into the Bible. Rather, we test our readings of the Bible in light of the creed. We do not assume that any particular biblical text teaches the creed per se, but we claim that, as a whole, the Bible is interpreted in a Christian fashion when our interpretations cohere with the creed. In the first century, the earliest creedal traditions (from the simple acclamation,

"Jesus is Lord" [1 Cor 12:3], to more developed statements like 1 Cor 15:3-5) served to unify the Christian movement and to clarify its faith in the context of its challengers. From the second century onward, these creedal traditions were formalized as creeds, like the Apostles' Creed or the Nicene Creed, and in this form continued to speak to the integrity of the Christian church and its faith. "The creed provides a measure or rule for the proper reading of Scripture. Such a rule is necessary for a coherent communal understanding of Scripture."[7]

In the case of Wesley, the analogy of faith took a particular form, structured as it was around the journey of salvation. Since he could assume that methodists were practicing members of the Church of England, and therefore affirmed the church's Articles of Religion, he was free to emphasize more narrowly the order of salvation: original sin, justification by faith and the new birth, and growth in holiness or sanctification. Whatever else we might expect of his reading of Revelation 21:1-5, then, we might assume that John's announcement that God "makes all things new" would be developed by Wesley in terms of the ultimate salvation of God's people.

We should reflect on what these two interpretive principles say about reading the Bible. We find here, first, an assumption that the Bible is a single book, even though it is actually a collection of sixty-six books. Written over a lengthy period of time, by disparate writers and editors, to address different aims among God's people, these books nevertheless comprise one book, speaking with the one voice of its divine Author, God. Hence, one can, as Wesley does, turn to Genesis or Romans or 2 Peter to make sense of Revelation. Second, the unity of Scripture is not so much inherent to the biblical materials themselves. This is because, as I have said, these materials speak in many voices, in many times, for many reasons. Instead, the unity of Scripture resides in the analogy of faith, itself taught by the whole of Scripture even though no particular text speaks in just that fashion.

As important as these two interpretive principles are for Wesley, a close reading of his sermon "The New Creation" reveals two further, perhaps equally important factors. The first is his dependence on the natural sciences, sometimes reflecting ancient views of the world and sometimes interacting in the sermon itself with views that would have been contemporary to Wesley. Here we see him putting into play what the Christian tradition has often called "God's Two Books," Scripture and the natural world. In this formulation, both are revelatory of God and God's purpose, even if Scripture's witness was the more sharply focused of the two. Wesley does not struggle with the relationship between Scripture and science in this sermon, but uses science to shape his understanding of what "a new heaven and a new earth" must entail.

Second, just as numerous interpreters, Wesley among them, depended more on Dante's *Inferno* than on Scripture for their portraits of hell, so Wesley depends in this sermon on Milton's *Paradise Lost* for his portrait of heaven. Although we have good reason to think that both Dante and Milton have gone beyond the witness of Scripture in their respective portraits of the destinations of the wicked and the righteous, we should not be surprised that Wesley finds in such imaginative, poetic representations the help that he needs to grapple with John's "strange scene," "so remote from all our natural apprehensions."

Returning to the sermon itself, Wesley first rejects those interpretations of Revelation 21 that downplay its end-time focus. He condemns any thought that John's vision concerns the present day: "What a miserable way is this of making void the whole counsel of God" (§4).

Although John uses the singular "heaven" in 21:1, Genesis 1 has "heavens," and this plural form appears widely throughout the Bible. Wesley takes his cue from this wider usage in order to document the transformation of "the heavens." Noting that Jewish thought upheld the notion of "three heavens" (even if Jewish writers actually held different views on heaven's "levels"), Wesley interprets each. The third heaven is God's abode and requires no transformation. The second is the "starry heaven," which, based on his reading of 2 Peter 3, Wesley regards as destined for obliteration in preparation for a "universal restoration that is to succeed the universal destruction" (§7). This new (second) heaven will lack the chaos of comets and half-formed planets, and instead will be characterized by harmony and order. Following the ancient astronomers, he reads the first heaven as the earth and its air. Using ancient categories, Wesley documents how each of the four elements of this "heaven" will undergo transformation (§§9–16): air ("only pleasing, healthful breezes"), fire ("it will forget its power to burn"), water ("clear and limpid, pure from all unpleasing or unhealthful mixtures"), and earth (no earthquakes or volcanoes, no thorns or thistles, no weeds or poisonous plants, "no impassable morasses or unfaithful bogs"). And, Wesley enthuses, all of this has to do only with the inanimate creation.

What of the animal world? As great a transformation of the rest of creation, "it is little, it is nothing, in comparison with what will then take place throughout all animated nature" (§17). Due to human sin, creation has suffered. Indeed, as a result of human sin,

> how many millions of creatures in the sea, in the air, and on every part of the earth, can now preserve their own lives only by taking away the lives of others; by tearing into pieces and devouring their poor, innocent, unresisting fellow-creatures! Miserable lot of such innumerable multitudes, who, insignificant as they seem, are the offspring of one common Father, the creatures of the same God of love!

Wesley continues, "But it shall not always be so. He that sits on the throne will soon change the face of all things, and give a demonstrative proof to all his creatures that 'his mercy is over all his works.' "

> On the new earth no creature will kill or hurt or give pain to any other. The scorpion will have no poisonous sting, the adder no venomous teeth. The lion will have no claws to tear the lamb; no teeth to grind his flesh and bones. Indeed, no creature, no beast, bird, or fish, will have any inclination to hurt any other. For cruelty will be far away, and savageness and fierceness be forgotten. So that violence shall be heard no more, neither wasting or destruction seen on the face of the earth. "The wolf shall dwell with the lamb" ... "and the leopard shall lie down with the kid." "They shall not hurt or destroy," from the rising up of the sun to the going down of the same. (§17)

With these words, Wesley interprets what it means for the almighty God to proclaim, "See, I am making all things new." In its concluding paragraph his sermon reaches its climax by describing what this final transformation means for the human family:

> Hence will arise an unmixed state of holiness and happiness far superior to what Adam enjoyed in paradise. In how beautiful and affecting a manner is this described by the apostle! "God shall wipe away all tears from their eyes; and there shall be no more death, neither sorrow nor crying, neither shall there be any more pain: for the former things are done away." As there will be no more death, and no more pain or sickness . . . ; as there will be no more grieving for or parting with friends; so there will be no more sorrow or crying. There will be a greater deliverance than all this; for there will be no more sin. And to crown all, there will be a deep, an intimate, an uninterrupted union with God; a constant communion with the Father and his Son Jesus Christ, through the Spirit; a continual enjoyment of the Three-One God, and of all the creatures in him!

Indeed, what a remarkable scene John has given us—not in order to feed curiosity or nurture speculation about the end, but in order to cultivate hope in the God who will set things right, and to call for present responses of faithfulness and praise. This vision has its proper effect if it results in our worship, and Charles Wesley has given us words to shape our praise:

> Finish then thy new creation,
> Pure and spotless let us be;
> Let us see thy great salvation
> Perfectly restored in thee;
> Changed from glory into glory,
> Till in heaven we take our place,
> Till we cast our crowns before thee,
> Lost in wonder, love, and praise.[8]

Questions for Reflection and Discussion

1. Revelation tells us that our actions have real and eternal consequences. Looking at your life now, what are the short and

long-term consequences of the life you are leading? If you keep going in the direction you are going now, where will you end up? Where will you be in ten or twenty years? Where will your church be?

2. When God looks at you, who does God see? When God looks at your church, what might God see?

3. The symbol of Jesus as the Lamb of God is powerful and striking. What does it mean to you? What does it say about God?

4. Revelation has a message to churches that practice idolatry and immorality. What idols do churches worship today: tradition, the past, money, my family, the way we've always done it, a particular pastor or teacher, a certain worship style, or others? How can we bring our church back to worshiping God alone? What immoralities plague our churches: lying, gossip, overindulgence, anger, greed, envy, laziness, pride? How can we align our church's purpose with God's?

5. Revelation reminds us that following Jesus can be a costly and risky business. Yet, following Jesus is also exciting and worth it all. How excited are you to be a Christian? How risk-averse are you?

6. How would the world look if it was truly aligned with God's purpose? How would your church look? How would your life look?

7. Think of a time when you were moved beyond words or that something significant touched you deeply. Reflect on your most recent experience of being in God's presence.

8. Christ will have the final victory. He will be a good winner. What does that mean? Reflect on a time when you or someone you know was magnanimous in victory.

Notes

Introduction

1. I refer to "methodists" with a lowercase "m" deliberately, in order to draw attention to a theological and ecclesial tradition without referring more narrowly to a particular denomination.

2. John Wesley, *Advice to the People Called Methodists with Regard to Dress*, §5.1.

3. John Wesley, *Farther Thoughts on Christian Perfection*.

4. John Wesley, "On God's Vineyard," §1.1.

5. John Wesley, Preface to *Sermons on Several Occasions*, §5.

6. In a letter to William Dodd, dated 5 February 1756, Wesley adds an important nuance to this claim: "In 1730, I began to be *homo unius libri*, to study (comparatively) no book but the Bible."

1. Gospel of Matthew

1. "St. Mark in his Gospel presupposes that of St. Matthew, and supplies what is omitted therein. St. Luke supplies what is omitted by both the former; St. John, what is omitted by all the three" (John Wesley, *Explanatory Notes upon the New Testament* [London: Epworth, 1976 (1754)], 11).

2. See, e.g., Richard A. Burridge, *Four Gospels, One Jesus: A Symbolic Reading* (2nd ed.; Grand Rapids: Eerdmans, 2005).

3. Wesley, *Explanatory Notes*, 16.

4. Ibid., 22.

5. Ibid., 53.

6. "A Plain Account of the People Called Methodists," §XII.2.

7. Wesley, *Explanatory Notes*, 37.

8. Ibid., 90.

9. See also Wesley's Sermon 65, "The Duty of Reproving Our Neighbour," on Leviticus 19:17, in which he wrote, "If we do not hate them in our heart, if we love our neighbor as ourselves, this will be our constant endeavor—to warn them of every evil way and of every mistake that tends to evil" (§I.2).

10. Wesley, *Explanatory Notes*, 35, 41.

2. Gospel of Mark

1. That is, Mark seems "to condense" or "to give an abridgement" of Matthew's Gospel; the Latin term is *breviator*.
2. For a brief introduction to the history of interpretation of Mark, see W. R. Telford, *The Theology of the Gospel of Mark* (New Testament Theology; Cambridge: Cambridge University Press, 1999), 214–17. See also Thomas C. Oden and Christopher A. Hall, *Mark* (Ancient Christian Commentary on Scripture: New Testament 2; Downers Grove, Ill.: InterVarsity, 1998).
3. Wesley, *Explanatory Notes*, 11.
4. Wesley, "On Working out Our Own Salvation," §3.2.
5. See Wesley, "The Repentance of Believers," §2.
6. Wesley knew Greek, of course, and in his comments on Luke 17:21 acknowledges the alternative translation: "*within*, or among, *you*" (*Explanatory Notes*, 269; the italicized words are from the AV).
7. Wesley, *Explanatory Notes*, 22.
8. See, e.g., Mark 1:2-3; 4:4, 15; 6:8; 8:3, 27; 9:33-34; 10:17, 32, 46, 52; 11:8.
9. This evangelist "may very probably think in a different manner from us even on several subjects of importance, such as the nature and use of the moral law, the eternal decrees of God, the sufficiency and efficacy of his grace, and the perseverance of his children" (II.3).
10. Wesley, *Explanatory Notes*, 171.
11. See further, Wesley, "Catholic Spirit."

3. Gospel of Luke

1. Wesley, *Explanatory Notes*, 196, 392. See further, below, chap. 5.
2. See Joel B. Green, "Good News to Whom? Jesus and the 'Poor' in the Gospel of Luke," in *Jesus of Nazareth: Lord and Christ. Essays on the Historical Jesus and New Testament Christology* (ed. Joel B. Green and Max Turner; Grand Rapids: Eerdmans, 1994), 59–74.
3. E.g., Acts 9:2; 19:9, 23; 22:4; 24:14, 22.
4. Albert C. Outler, "Introduction," in *The Works of John Wesley*, vol. 1: *Sermons—I (1-33)* (ed. Albert C. Outler; Nashville: Abingdon, 1984), 1–100 (69).
5. I should add, though, that I have chosen the word *handbook* deliberately, rather than, say, *encyclopedia*. This is because Wesley's comments are sparse, he does not often deal with the different opinions of his background sources, and he has his own biases about first-century Jewish life that sometimes get in the way of his reading.
6. For a similar judgment, see Robin Scroggs, "John Wesley as Biblical Scholar," *Journal of Bible and Religion* 28 (1960): 415–22 (418).
7. Wesley, "Preface," in *Sermons on Several Occasions*, §5.
8. See Wilbur H. Mullen, "John Wesley's Method of Biblical Interpretation," *Religion in Life* 47 (1978): 99–108 (102).
9. Wesley, "Preface," in *Sermons on Several Occasions*, §3.

10. Wesley, *Explanatory Notes,* 200.

11. Ibid., 202.

12. Ibid., 240.

13. Ibid., 288.

14. The title of the Latin original is *Gnomon Novi Testamenti.* For background on Bengel, see W. R. Baird, "Bengel, Johann Albrecht," in *Dictionary of Biblical Interpretation* (2 vols.; ed. John H. Hayes; Nashville: Abingdon, 1999), 1:120. On Wesley's use of Bengel and others, see the helpful summary in Scroggs, "Biblical Scholar," 415–19.

15. *"Penichros"* ("poor") appears in the New Testament only in Luke 21:2; and *"ptōchos"* ("poor") appears 10 times in Luke, 5 in Matthew, 5 in Mark, 4 in John, 4 in Paul's letters, 4 in James, and 2 in Revelation.

16. See Dennis J. Ireland, *Stewardship and the Kingdom of God: An Historical, Exegetical, and Contextual Study of the Parable of the Unjust Steward in Luke 16:1-13* (Supplements to Novum Testamentum 70; Leiden: Brill, 1992).

4. Gospel of John

1. The Gospel of Luke has Jesus in Jerusalem shortly after his birth and again at age twelve (Luke 2:22-52), but only once, at the end, as an adult.

2. This paraphrase attempts to draw out the significance of the contrast Clement makes between *ta sōmatika* (provided by the Synoptic Gospels) and *pneumatikon* (his description of the Fourth Gospel). The contrast suggested by some interpreters of Clement, between "bodily" or "physical" and "spiritual," helps us little.

3. Origen, *Commentary on John,* 10.2.

4. Ibid., 10.16.

5. Wesley, *Explanatory Notes,* 310.

6. Ibid., 300.

7. Ibid., 302.

8. Translation from Joel B. Green, *1 Peter* (Two Horizons Commentary on the New Testament; Grand Rapids: Eerdmans, 2007), 21.

9. Wesley, *Explanatory Notes,* 311.

10. Ibid., 312.

11. John Wesley, *Farther Thoughts on Christian Perfection.*

12. Brevard S. Childs, "Toward Recovering Theological Exegesis," *Pro Ecclesia 6* (1997): 16–26 (20).

13. Paraphrase from "The New Birth," §II.4, in John Wesley, *The New Birth: A Modern English Edition* (ed. Thomas C. Oden; San Francisco: Harper & Row, 1984), 9.

14. Ibid., 11.

5. Acts of the Apostles

1. Wesley, *Explanatory Notes,* 392.

2. See Isaiah 8:9; 45:22; 48:20; 62:11.

3. Wesley, *Explanatory Notes,* 396.

4. Ibid., 397.

5. Ibid., 402, 409.

6. Romans

1. Wesley, *Explanatory Notes,* 513. Strangely, Wesley also refers to "both the treatises of St. Luke," presumably because both the Gospel of Luke and the Acts of the Apostles refer to Luke's literary patron, Theophilus, in their prefaces. This identification of Luke and Acts as "epistles" plays no role at all in Wesley's interpretation of these books, however.

2. See, for example, the recent attempt of Thomas C. Oden to organize a kind of compendium of Wesley's thought in terms of the major loci of Christian theology in *John Wesley's Scriptural Christianity: A Plain Exposition of His Teaching on Christian Doctrine* (Grand Rapids: Zondervan, 1994); or Kenneth J. Collins's articulation of Wesley's theology in *The Theology of John Wesley: Holy Love and the Shape of Grace* (Nashville: Abingdon, 2007).

3. Wesley, *Explanatory Notes,* 513.

4. Melanchthon, *Loci Communes;* quoted in Eduard Schweizer, "The Church as the Missionary Body of Christ," *New Testament Studies* 8 (1961–62): 1–11 (1).

5. Wesley, *Explanatory Notes,* 514.

6. Ibid., 582.

7. Robert Jewett, *Romans* (Hermeneia; Minneapolis: Fortress, 2007), 974. See further, Emerson B. Powery, "Kiss," in *The New Interpreter's Dictionary of the Bible* (5 vols.; ed. Katharine Doob Sakenfeld; Nashville: Abingdon, 2006–9), 3:536.

7. 1–2 Corinthians

1. Wesley, *Explanatory Notes,* 584.

2. Ibid., 643.

3. The Jackson edition also includes "On the Resurrection of the Dead" (1 Cor 15:35) and "On the Holy Spirit" (2 Cor 3:17).

4. Wesley, *Explanatory Notes,* 657.

5. Ibid.

8. Hebrews

1. Outler, "Introduction," 69.

2. Wesley, *Explanatory Notes,* 808.

3. Ibid., 809.

4. Ibid., 824.

5. Ibid., 853.

6. Wesley, "Nature, Design, and Rules of the United Societies," §2.

9. James and 1 Peter

1. Wesley, *Explanatory Notes,* 856.
2. Ibid., 857.
3. Ibid., 871.
4. Translation from Green, *1 Peter,* 14.
5. Translation from the Loeb Classical Library.
6. John Wesley, "Predestination Calmly Considered," §9.
7. John Wesley, "Free Grace," §9.
8. Wesley, *Explanatory Notes,* 872.
9. Wesley, "On Predestination," §5.
10. Wesley, *Explanatory Notes,* 872.

10. 1 John

1. John Wesley, "The Witness of the Spirit—Discourse One," §I.4.
2. Scott J. Jones fixes the number of references at 438 (*John Wesley's Conception and Use of Scripture* [Nashville: Abingdon, 1995], 226).
3. Wesley, *Explanatory Notes,* 902.
4. Ibid., 913.
5. Ibid.

11. Revelation

1. Wesley, *Explanatory Notes,* 22.
2. Ibid., 932.
3. Ibid., 1000; see 1000–1012.
4. See further, Revelation 1:10-20; 2:1, 8, 12, 18; 3:1, 7, 14; 10:8-10; 19:9; 22:7, 9-10, 18-19.
5. C. S. Lewis, *The Magician's Nephew* (New York: Macmillan, 1970), 125.
6. James Wm. McClendon Jr., *Systematic Theology,* vol. 3: *Witness* (Nashville: Abingdon, 2000), 358–62 (362); I have adapted the version of the American Story that McClendon recounts.
7. Luke Timothy Johnson, *The Creed: What Christians Believe and Why It Matters* (New York: Doubleday, 2003), 47.
8. Charles Wesley, "Love Divine, All Loves Excelling," *United Methodist Hymnal* (Nashville: United Methodist Publishing House, 1989 [1747]), no. 384.

Bibliography

Baird, W. R. "Bengel, Johann Albrecht." In *Dictionary of Biblical Interpretation*, 2 vols., ed. John H. Hayes, 1:120. Nashville: Abingdon, 1999.

Burridge, Richard A. *Four Gospels, One Jesus: A Symbolic Reading*. 2nd ed. Grand Rapids: Eerdmans, 2005.

Childs, Brevard S. "Toward Recovering Theological Exegesis." *Pro Ecclesia* 6 (1997): 16–26.

Collins, Kenneth J. *The Theology of John Wesley: Holy Love and the Shape of Grace*. Nashville: Abingdon, 2007.

Green, Joel B. "Good News to Whom? Jesus and the 'Poor' in the Gospel of Luke." In *Jesus of Nazareth: Lord and Christ. Essays on the Historical Jesus and New Testament Christology*, ed. Joel B. Green and Max Turner, 59–74. Grand Rapids: Eerdmans, 1994.

————. *1 Peter*. Two Horizons New Testament Commentary. Grand Rapids: Eerdmans, 2007.

Jewett, Robert. *Romans*. Hermeneia. Minneapolis: Fortress, 2007.

Johnson, Luke Timothy. *The Creed: What Christians Believe and Why It Matters*. New York: Doubleday, 2003.

Jones, Scott J. *John Wesley's Conception and Use of Scripture*. Nashville: Abingdon, 1995.

Lewis, C. S. *The Magician's Nephew*. New York: Macmillan, 1970.

McClendon, James Wm., Jr. *Systematic Theology*, vol. 3: *Witness*. Nashville: Abingdon, 2000.

Mullen, Wilbur H. "John Wesley's Method of Biblical Interpretation." *Religion in Life* 47 (1978): 99–108.

Oden, Thomas C. *John Wesley's Scriptural Christianity: A Plain Exposition of His Teaching on Christian Doctrine*. Grand Rapids: Zondervan, 1994.

Oden, Thomas C., and Christopher A. Hall. *Mark*. Ancient Christian Commentary on Scripture: New Testament 2. Downers Grove, Ill.: InterVarsity, 1998.

Outler, Albert C. "Introduction." In *The Works of John Wesley*, vol. 1: *Sermons—I (1–33)*, ed. Albert C. Outler, 1–100. Nashville: Abingdon, 1984.

Powery, Emerson B. "Kiss." In *The New Interpreter's Dictionary of the Bible*, 5 vols., edited by Katharine Doob Sakenfeld, 3:536. Nashville: Abingdon, 2006–9.

Schweizer, Eduard. "The Church as the Missionary Body of Christ." *New Testament Studies* 8 (1961–62): 1–11.

Scroggs, Robin. "John Wesley as Biblical Scholar." *Journal of Bible and Religion* 28 (1960): 415–22.

Telford, W. R. *The Theology of the Gospel of Mark.* New Testament Theology. Cambridge: Cambridge University Press, 1999.

Wesley, Charles. "Love Divine, All Loves Excelling." *United Methodist Hymnal,* no. 384. Nashville: United Methodist Publishing House, 1989 [1747].

Wesley, John. *Explanatory Notes upon the New Testament.* London: Epworth, 1976 (1754).

———. *The New Birth: A Modern English Edition.* Edited by Thomas C. Oden. San Francisco: Harper & Row, 1984.

———. *The Works of John Wesley.* Bicentennial Edition. Nashville: Abingdon, 1980–.

Scripture Index